From A Small Town
To The World

From A Small Town To The World

MY STORY

Dr. David L. Stratmon, Sr.

To order additional copies of this book, contact:
Xlibris Corporation
1-888-795-4274
www.Xlibris.com
Orders@Xlibris.com
47530

Contents

PART II

PART III

Dedication

This book is dedicated to my wife, Lillian Jean, whose love and encouragement sustained me.

Foreword

I had the privilege of meeting David L. Stratmon at his aunt's home (Mrs. Eva Virginia Lee) in Southport (population 1,500) in Brunswick County, North Carolina. His aunt and uncle, Eva and Charles W. Lee, were my foster parents. David was the youngest boy in the neighborhood group of friends; therefore, he was usually left behind when it came to running and swimming. Although he was the youngest, he was acknowledged as the brightest.

His aunt and uncle often said he would excel in school and in the workplace. Possibly, they had a glimpse of the future because their prediction came true. Following his graduation at the head of his class from Brunswick County Training School in Southport, he finished college at Howard University and completed his doctoral degree at the University of Michigan without receiving any financial aid from home. In fact, David made education a lifelong experience by constantly studying. Because he took education seriously, he was rewarded with an amazing career as a diplomat which took him all over the world. After retiring from the diplomatic world, he shared his experiences with young adults as a teacher at Rust College in Holly Springs, Mississippi. In addition, his role as a community leader in Holly Springs enriched the quality of life in that small town.

He was reared by his grandmother and other relatives. Early on, he was captivated by his grandfather, Mr. Frank Gordon, who was the first black teacher in Brunswick County. Mr. Frank, as we called him, was thought to be the most brilliant man in the county. Perhaps, this was the inspiration which sparked the qualities that made David push himself at a time that was very difficult for little black children and adults. My friends and I referred to him as the dreamer. Even as a young boy, we thought of him as persistent, honest, dedicated, and driven.

Dr. David L. Stratmon was a man of the hour who made the world a better place for human beings. This biography will be inspirational, informational, and encouraging to the young as well as mature citizens of all classes and ethnic groups.

W. A. McMillan, President Emeritus
Rust College, Holly Springs, MS

Acknowledgments

I would like to acknowledge the following people
for assisting me in the creation of this book: my wife,
Lillian Jean, for her editorial skills and encouragement
in supporting the book and for her perseverance and
fortitude in getting it published, and Dr. Debayo Moyo
for his expertness in using computer programs
for improving old photographs.
Thank you very much.

FROM A SMALL TOWN TO THE WORLD

Introduction

There were times when I could have given up on writing my memoirs, put my papers away, and logged off my computer. But the thoughts of future generations, students of history, my former classmates, and especially my family made me continue. Just as I wondered about the thoughts, the experiences, the joys, and the triumphs of my ancestors, someone else may wonder about me. I hope to answer their questions.

Historians might like to know how a little poor barefoot black boy could come out of high school in a remote part of North Carolina, achieve a higher education in Michigan, and travel around the world as a diplomat. They might want to know about the historical and social framework that pervaded during my formative and most productive years. I will attempt to explain this. Much of the information is pieced together from programs, records, and other documents which I saved. I did not keep a journal; but I am pretty well documented through various records, reports, and articles. These back up my professional experiences very well. For my early life in North Carolina, I relied on interviews with relatives, classmates (yes, some classmates were still around at the time of this writing), friends, and memory.

I'll begin in chapter 1 by reviewing my early years. High school experiences and jobs that I held around that time at the Southport Hospital and Hotel Bame are revisited. People who were my special mentors such as my Grandma Mame, Aunt Nannie, Great-grandfather Frank C. Gordon, and Great-grandpa Miles Bryant are discussed. In chapter 2, I review my post-high school educational activities at places such as North Carolina A&T University, Howard University, the University of Michigan, the Arabic Language School, the National War College, and Georgetown University Law Center.

Throughout the discussion, items are not in chronological order because of the way I have grouped them. Many events occurred between the times I went from North Carolina A&T University to Georgetown Law Center, but since they are both educational institutions, they are in the same chapter. All of the years are included, so readers will be able to follow along as the blanks are filled in later chapters. Service in the US Army is reviewed in chapter 3, and time spent as a US information officer is examined in chapter 4. I have six children, four adopted from various countries and two stepchildren, which you will read about in chapter 5. My stint at Prairie View A&M University is explored in chapter 6, and then we look at the time I spent serving the country as a US Foreign Service information officer. Finally, chapter 15 contains information about my post-foreign service activities, and chapter 16 reveals my long-held opinions. The journey begins with the early years.

PART I

Chapter 1

Early Years

What pervades the memory of my early years was the abject poverty. The fact that I was deserted by my mother at two years old was painful, and the resulting poverty was excruciating. Getting away from it was a goal I set as a very young child. Here is an account of how I began that lifelong process.

Childhood

Eloise Gordon, my mother, married James William "Willie" Stratmon around 1922; and they had two children. James Oliver Stratmon was born sometime in May 1923. I was born March 20, 1925, and I was named David Leander. I never knew Willie because he died six months before I was born.

James William Stratmon, father of David and James
Stratmon, died in 1924, six months before David was born

Folks said he was a cook on a boat. I don't know where he worked,
but it might have been in Southport, North Carolina, since Southport
is a seaport town. I didn't know Eloise either because she asked my
grandmother to keep James and me, then she left. I guess leaving two
small children behind must have been hard for her; it was traumatic
for James and me. The two of us, along with our young cousin, used to
climb onto the fence in the yard and try to get her to return by yelling,
"Doll, come home. Doll, please come home." My grandmother and
other relatives referred to Eloise as "Doll," so I called her "Doll" too. Our
young voices probably weren't strong enough to be heard in Florida,
because she didn't answer us. I was fourteen when I saw her again. It
was at James's high school graduation ceremony.

Various relatives told me that Eloise went to Florida to marry a man
named William Hunter by whom she had three children: Mabel Mary

Evelyn, Emily, and one boy, Clyde. I saw my three sisters for the first time when they accompanied Eloise to Southport for James's graduation. I met Clyde for the first time when I drove with my family from Ann Arbor, Michigan, where I attended graduate school, to New Smyrna Beach, Florida, to visit my mother and her family in the early 1950s.

Eloise Gordon, mother of David and James Stratmon

Certainly, times for black folks were exceedingly hard everywhere in those days. Perhaps Eloise left us because she knew that she did not have the means to support us, and there was no welfare in those days. When I finally saw her, I wanted some kind of explanation, but I guess that was too much for her. The fact that she failed to try to rationalize her decision left me with a good deal of resentment. As years passed, I managed to overcome my anger by providing my own rationalizations.

We were hungry much of the time, and we were treated poorly most of the time. We lived in a house on Howe Street in Southport with my cousins, the McCoys. Since the McCoys owned the house, they required that my brother and I always enter the back door. My cousin, who was my age, could go through the front door. We could see the neighbors peering through their windows as James and I went around back while Charles Nelson McCoy, my cousin and playmate, entered the front door. As a matter of fact, all the McCoys used the front door and all the Gordons used the back door, and there were a lot of people in the Gordon family. When we got inside the house, we could be seen from the living room as we ascended the stairs to our rooms. To avoid the dilemma of being spotted by nosy people, Joseph McCoy had the stairway rebuilt so that we could enter and exit without being seen by anyone sitting in the parlor or in the front part of the house. This became a constant reminder of who the McCoys were and who we were.

Years later, there was a family reunion in New Smyrna, Florida, where I heard many stories of family triumphs and tribulations. I made tape recordings of those stories. I will share some of them with you throughout the chapters.

High School

By studying diligently, I was able to make good grades in each of my high school courses. By the time I reached my senior year in 1941, I was sixteen years old, and I felt I had a hammerlock on the top honors in my graduating class. I was not surprised when Mr. A. C. Caviness, the principal, called me into his office and told me that I should begin to prepare a valedictory address for the upcoming commencement program. We did not have a debating team at Brunswick County Training School (BCTS)BCT*See* Brunswick County Training School in Southport, but I had gained a little experience in public speaking, and I practiced well before that awesome graduation day rolled around. By working hard, I was able to memorize my speech; and thereby, I got through it without making a fool of myself in front of the many family members, friends, teachers, community leaders, and fellow students.

Although I graduated as valedictorian of the class of 1941, I had no money for college. Despite that, we were fortunate enough to have had a remarkable high school principal, Mr. Caviness. Each Friday, he repeated the story at assembly of how he had attended Johnson C. Smith University in Charlotte, North Carolina, by working at odd jobs. His purpose for drumming this message into our heads was to make us feel that our poverty was no excuse for not going to college. Our homeroom teachers, most of whom Mr. Caviness personally recruited, all emphasized the same upbeat message. Poverty was no excuse for not getting a college education though times were especially hard during the Depression years and immediately thereafter.

One result of these pep talks by Mr. Caviness and our teachers was that seven of the ten boys in my graduating class completed at least four years of college and became teachers. Some of the girls decided to get married soon after graduation, but most of them eventually completed college and became teachers as well.

In those days, none of my classmates had ever heard of illegal drugs, other than corn whiskey. Even then, we did not think it was smart to drink whiskey. We didn't want to risk becoming a town drunk as opposed to becoming a successful college graduate.

Southport Hospital

After high school graduation, I gave up my newspaper route which I had held for a long time. Then I began my stint as a dishwasher at the local hospital. Pay as a dishwasher was very low, even by prevailing standards in the area in 1941, but I gladly took the job, and I cleaned those dishes really well because I wanted to keep it. But I continued to keep my ear to the ground to see if I could find better employment.

I felt overwhelmed because I did not have any money to enter college that fall following graduation. Ironically, I was a high school valedictorian, and yet I had no scholarship offers. Notwithstanding, my grandmother constantly encouraged me to work hard, to save every penny from the dishwashing job, and to enter college in the spring semester of 1942. That became my game plan, and the plan worked.

While working as a dishwasher, I received a summons from Dr. J. Arthur Dosher one day. He had been the doctor who delivered me from my mother's womb sixteen years earlier. One day, Dr. Dosher told me to wash my hands and come to the operating room. He was about to perform surgery on a patient. He told me to hold the patient's left leg steady and straight while he attached a metal plate to hold the broken leg bone in place. With that short explanation, the doctor signaled the anesthesiologist to administer the medication needed to put the patient to sleep. Then the bloody operation began.

Although I had never witnessed an operation before, I must have done a pretty good job of holding the leg in place. Shortly after that, I was told that my duties would include administering shots once a week to male patients from the colored community who showed up for their weekly syphilis shots. A nurse showed me how to administer the shot, and all I had to do was to wait for patients. When male adults from the area came in and found that a teenager had been assigned to give them shots, they seemed embarrassed and ill at ease. However, after making jokes about the size of the needle I was about to stick into their hind quarters, they all pulled down their britches, gritted their teeth, and thanked me for giving them the required medicine.

I was surprised to find that although many men from the Southport community came regularly for their syphilis shots, their wives and girlfriends were not treated. I wondered what good it would do to treat only husbands and provide no treatment for their wives and girlfriends. Realistically though, I was merely the dishwasher who happened to be called upon to give shots. So I kept my opinions to myself and held on to that job until I was ready to leave.

Another job of mine at the hospital was to take all of the bloody linens from the operating room down to the kitchen and wash them in cold water. After that, I would hang them on the line to dry. The hospital did not have a dryer in those days. I did as I was told, while at the same time worrying about the wisdom of washing bloody linen in the same large container into which water from the dishwasher was drained. Nobody seemed to be concerned about the possibility of cross contamination.

In those days, the scourge of AIDS had not yet appeared, and probably none of the medical personnel felt that there was any danger in recycling the operating-room linen by merely giving it a good rinsing with cold water to remove bloodstains. Though I washed with my hands frequently, I was not given rubber gloves to use for scrubbing the operating-room linen in the kitchen facility. That is the way things were done then.

Hotel Bame

After a few months of working at the Southport Hospital, Richard Griffin, one of my high school classmates, told me that Hotel Bame located in Carolina Beach, North Carolina, had an opening for a dishwasher. I caught the Atlantic Coastline bus in Wilmington and rode down to the beach to apply for the job. I was hired and told that I could start work right away.

My job was to use a dishwashing machine to keep up with the mountain of dishes left behind after the hotel's three daily meals were served. In addition, I was told to sit on the end of the front porch when not washing dishes and help guests with their luggage when they arrived at the hotel.

Hotel Bame gave its employees a place to sleep and three meals each day, and it had a pleasant work environment. I enjoyed the work in part because I was able to save almost every penny of my pay. I planned to use this little nest egg to help pay college tuition. My little pile of money soon added up to enough to pay all the tuition required by the Agricultural and Mechanical College at Greensboro, North Carolina.

There was even enough left over to pay for a round-trip train ticket from Wilmington to Greensboro.

Grandma Mame

This section is mostly about one person, but I must say a few words about another remarkable lady who played a major role in my upbringing. Though I will discuss other relatives in this section, it will mainly be about two women. The two women are my maternal grandmother, Mame (Mary Martha McCoy Gordon), and one of Mame's seven children by Cenelius Gordon, namely, Aunt Nannie (Nannie Evelyn Gordon). I will say more about Aunt Nannie later.

Mame wore cotton dresses – frocks, as she called them – which were faded, but "store bought." On Sunday, she would put on the best of the lot of those nondescript cotton dresses after someone helped her squeeze into her whalebone corset. She always wore that whalebone corset on Sunday. Right after my return home from the St. James African Methodist Episcopal Zion Church service on Sundays, Mame would quiz me about the subject of the preacher's sermon. I can still remember, "What scripture reading did he select to go with his text?" Because of this frequent examination, I always paid very careful attention when the preacher announced the topic of his sermon and what chapter(s) and verse(s) of the Bible he was going to use to develop his message. It's my belief that Mame got out her Bible and read the verses that I told her about, and she probably reflected on those passages after we had eaten our late-afternoon meal.

Grandma Mame raised me from the time I turned two years old, and I think she did a pretty good job. My system of values is mainly Mame's – with a dash of Nannie's homespun wisdom added. Mame had a sense of humor. She took the long view when things were going badly. Mame believed that if you did not forget to pray, which she constantly reminded me in her letters as I traveled to many foreign countries during World War II, then everything will turn out okay.

Mame must have felt distressed about the way she was treated by her husband, Cenelius Gordon. He abandoned her after he fathered her seven children. My mother, Eloise, was one of those abandoned children. I found it interesting that she had been abandoned, and later, she did the same thing to two of her children. Through all this, I never heard Mame say anything critical about Cenelius. This led me to believe that if Cenelius had ever decided to return to Southport, Mame would have been glad to resume her long marriage with him as if nothing happened.

As fate would have it, Grandpa Cenelius never did come back alive. When he died, his body was returned from New York to Southport for burial. Since Mame showed no intention of paying him the honor of attending his funeral, I did not attend the funeral either. I hasten to add that I never knew Mame to attend church at all.

Mame always insisted that my brother, James Oliver, and I attend church. James was my senior by two years. We went to St. James African Methodist Episcopal Zion Church every Sunday, and we also participated in the Sunday school which started at 2:00 p.m. If asked to, I would help an adult class leader visit class members on Sunday afternoons to collect and record class dues. I always felt that the reason

Mame neither attended church nor attended her husband's funeral was because she did not own a single Sunday-go-to-meeting dress. She had only faded dresses that she wore during her daily chores around the house.

Mame was very human and down to earth. Nothing bears that out more vividly than the fact that on a hot day in Southport during the Depression years, Mame gave me what I, at first, thought was a very strange order. After a while, it was no longer "strange." First Mame and Aunt Florence, the youngest of her seven children, would wash and iron clothes for their white clients. Then I would balance the clothes basket on the handlebars of my bicycle and deliver them to the clients. Some of those clients were Mr. Jimmy Harper, Ms. Hattie Howell, and Mrs. Mary Thompson. Only after this process was completed would Mame take a handkerchief from her bosom which she kept carefully wrapped in white cloth, then she would take a dime from the cloth and say, "Run over to Dollie's and bring me a cold bottle of Atlantic Ale, David."

Mrs. Dollie Evans's grocery store was right across the street. I would dash across the two-lane asphalt road (later named Howe Street) and return with the cold eight-ounce bottle of beer concealed in a brown paper bag. Then I would linger around to watch my grandma as she opened the cold bottle of beer as she sat on the back porch of our house. She would try to beat the heat by savoring slow small sips gingerly taken from the brown bag which held the bottle with the long neck. I could tell that she was enjoying each swig. Her eyes seemed to take on a kind of mischievous twinkle as she relished each drop until the bottle was empty. But she never offered to let me take a drink from the bottle. Actually, I did not expect that she would because the consumption of alcohol by children was banned. As a matter of fact, it was absolutely frowned on by most of the elders in our family.

After Grandma Mame finished her bottle of Atlantic Ale beer, she would sit quietly in a relaxed mood for a while on the screened back porch. Eventually, she would tell me to put the empty bottle in the trash can. If I got a chance to do so without her seeing me, I would turn the bottle up to my mouth as I had observed her do in the past in an effort to see what there was about Atlantic Ale that was so special to my grandma. Alas, the dregs at the bottom of the bottle were always warm and bitter. I felt as though I had put cat hair in my mouth. So I had a hard time figuring out what grandma found so enjoyable about that beer.

Mame's older brother, Uncle Eddie (Edward E. "Bud" McCoy), was the no whiskey-drinking exception. He had served in the US Navy from 1906 to 1926 when he retired. We all knew that Uncle Eddie, "Our Bud" as Mame referred to him, usually invited some of his friends over to his small two-bedroom house located two doors down from our Howe Street house to help him guzzle down a few drinks. This was the way he celebrated when he received his pension check.

Uncle Eddie often provided store-bought whiskey, usually bourbon, for his guests on these celebratory occasions. Everybody made an exception for Bud, whom they viewed as the good-hearted retired sailor who drank whiskey in moderation. Though most respectable ladies and gentlemen in Southport frowned upon the practice of openly drinking whiskey at that time, what Bud McCoy and his friends did in private was overlooked. It was considered a private matter that did not offend public morals. He was free to have his monthly drinking parties and still remain a pillar of the St. James AMEZ Church.

Bud was an old sailor, and most old sailors were expected to "drink whiskey and chase skirts." So when Uncle Eddie engaged in these provocative activities, everybody turned a blind eye to him and condemned the practice among members of the community that they allowed for him. Bud McCoy joined the navy when he and one of his buddies wandered into the Philadelphia shipyard seeking employment. They were both employed immediately – as new recruits in the US Navy.

I don't want to give the impression that there was no discord surrounding Aunt Mame. On the contrary, there was plenty. Mrs. Viola "Oly" McCoy, Uncle Joseph McCoy's wife and Mame's sister-in-law, constantly nagged Grandma Mame. Cenelius, Mame's husband, had never bought a house for Mame. After all, he did desert her. Consequently, the McCoys had to share the family homestead with Mame and her children and their children. Mame, Oly, and Aunt Florence – Mame's youngest child – used the same wash shed every Monday morning. They had to launder clothes for our families, and they had to wash clothes that white families would drop off. All of this washing was done by hand using tin tubs, washboards, and big round iron pots. Mame made her own lye soap. This hard work and low pay must have been frustrating, notwithstanding problems with family dynamics.

Sometimes, Mame and Mrs. Oly could be seen facing each other while standing just a few feet apart, with Mrs. Oly sarcastically reminding Grandma Mame that "one day, every tub will have to stand on its own bottom." Mame never replied to the cruel, constant barbs. In fact, I never knew Oly and Mame to exchange even a "good morning" or a simple "hello" during all of the years I witnessed them living together in the same house. Mame always reminded me that the house was her house. She said that her father, Nelson McCoy, told her that he wanted her to have the house.

My great-granddad, Nelson McCoy, had not made his wishes clear. He said his young son, Joseph, should move out of the family homestead. He should have constructed a house for his family when he got married to Mrs. Oly. I guess Nelson assumed that Mame's husband, Cenelius Gordon, would never build a home for his family and their seven children. Grandma Mame's dad was right. Grandpa Cenelius always worked as a cook aboard large ships and was hardly ever in Southport. So he never got around to building a house for Mame and their three boys and four girls. Remember, one of those girls was Eloise Gordon-Stratmon, my mother.

It was extremely embarrassing for my brother and me when Mrs. Oly began to upgrade her insults. She added to her usual line of insults about the Gordons' living in the McCoy house. It went something like this: "Them boys [James and I] are too big to be sleeping in the room with Nannie." Nannie was one of the three aunts who shared the house with their mother, Mame, and her grandchildren. Additionally, there was the family of her younger brother, Joseph McCoy, and his family which included Uncle Joseph; his wife, Viola; and their two children, Josie Mae and Charles Nelson. Big, though crowded, the two-story frame house had two bedrooms on the first floor and four bedrooms on the second floor.

Mame would console the family and tell us to not pay any attention to what Oly said. Even so, it was still painful to be on the receiving end of the harsh tongue lashings from an aunt-in-law, Mrs. Oly. Even in the most difficult of social situations, such as the housing arrangement that we lived in for such a long time, Mame insisted that we must not lose our tempers. This went on from the time I was two until I reached sixteen years of age. At sixteen, I left home; and throughout life, Mame's maxim about controlling my temper has helped me avoid a lot of trouble.

Mame also taught me the value of honesty. We never had much money, but Mame drummed into my soul the commandment that you do not steal anything. One example was the instance when Mrs. Dollie Evans, our next-door neighbor, decided to provide pine bark for us. We needed it for our wood-burning stove located in an upstairs bedroom. Mame told me "in no uncertain terms" to load only bark on my cart and not a single piece of the pinewood that Mrs. Dollie used to sell as heating fuel. I am proud to say that I did just as I was told.

Mame preached that the only way a colored man was going to achieve anything in America was to get a good education. She made me understand that I had to take advantage of the wonderful free public education that was now available to each child in Southport. I decided that I must please my grandmother. By the time I entered first grade, I had set a goal to be at or near the top of my class. Thus, I graduated at sixteen years of age as class valedictorian. I had developed good study habits and a love of books.

Handouts from the government were something that Mame did not believe in. When some of the 1930s New Deal social programs under the Roosevelt administration began to trickle down to our small town, Mame spoke out. Mame told anyone who would listen that she did not want to receive any "poor relief" food or any other commodities from the government. Although we were as poor as "Job's turkey," as she described it, we would rather starve than seek a free handout from a poor-relief program. Middle-class folks like us did not need free handouts, and it was better to go hungry on occasion than to sink into that class of beggars who had to accept poor relief. Those were her firmly held convictions, and since she was the head of the family, I believed every word she said.

Since we did not "go on relief" and accept food from the government, we sometimes ran out of food. On occasion, this meant that we went to school after drinking a cup of weak tea and munching on a cold biscuit. We did not have an icebox to use for cooling our food. So occasionally some of the fish we ate tasted tainted, as if it were well on the way to spoiling. But eating tainted fish was far more appealing than the alternative of going to school or to bed hungry. In spite of this, we were very healthy.

Aunt Nannie

Nannie Evelyn Gordon was my mother's younger sister. When my mother left my brother and me in the care of Grandma Mame, Aunt Nannie was there to help out. I do not remember hearing Aunt Nannie say any unkind word about our mother, even though she left us without one penny of support. After I grew up and visited my mother in New Smyrna Beach, Florida, it became clear that she did not have the means to send anything. I believe that she would have been glad to send financial assistance had she not been so poor. The truth is that she lived most of her life in Florida at or below the poverty level.

Nannie's economic picture was just a little different. She made roughly $3.75 a week for as long as I can remember, and that was from childhood until 1942 when I left for college. Aunt Nannie worked as a domestic. She cooked and cleaned house at Mrs. Hattie Howell's boardinghouse on the waterfront in Southport. Nannie managed that small sum of money well. Early on, she opened an account at the building and loan association, and every week she deposited at least twenty-five cents in that account. From her one-dollar-a-month savings account, Nannie would splurge each Saturday night. She would send me "catty-cornered" across the street to Ms. Dollie Evans's general grocery store to purchase a ten-cent pickled pig's foot. I can still taste that mouthwatering delicacy if I close my eyes. Nannie would always break off a piece of the meat as a reward for my quick return from the store. It tasted mighty good.

After Nannie put her quarter in the bank and purchased her Saturday-night pickled pig foot, she would help feed the rest of the family by contributing money to Mame to help feed the family. Since Nannie ate almost all of her meals at the boardinghouse where she worked, she did not have to do this. Out of the goodness of her heart, she contributed to our support and care.

Years later, we were surprised to learn how consistent Nannie had been. I had completed college and started working for the federal government as a foreign service information officer when Nannie died. Everyone in the family was surprised when we found out that Nannie had saved enough money to pay for her final expenses and have a little left over. She left the remainder of her savings to her younger sister, Florence.

Aunt Nannie was generous to a fault. My brother and I often were on the receiving end of Nannie's generosity. In addition to helping keep food on the table from which everybody except Nannie ate, she would use part of her weekly salary to purchase clothes for James and me. This included buying new clothes to wear at the beginning of each school year. In the middle of one cold winter, James and I had only lightweight sweaters to wear to school and church. Nannie somehow arranged to purchase heavy fleece-lined three-quarter-length coats for us from a downtown store. She most certainly must have paid something into the layaway plan each week until she paid the entire balance. I do not think she tapped into her building and loan fund to make the purchase. We were delirious with joy when Nannie came home one Saturday night carrying those warm and beautiful coats. We could hardly wait for Monday to arrive so that we could wear them to school and make our friends envious.

Nannie's pleasures were simple. I never knew her to drink alcoholic beverages, smoke cigarettes, or even buy fancy clothes for herself. Instead, she seemed pleased that she was able to work and help keep food on the table for her nieces and nephews. But Nannie did allow herself to purchase a new frock or a pair of new shoes from the Sears Roebuck catalogue once in a while. By making these purchases, Nannie ensured that Sears Roebuck would continue to mail their annual catalogue to her. She always enjoyed sitting on the porch of our house and going slowly through the catalogue, pausing occasionally to exchange greetings with passersby along the street. Hardly any black person had a car in those days, so greetings were always exchanged whenever you passed a house where someone was sitting on the front porch.

Nannie liked to stroll through the forest in the fall of the year. She would call to me and say, "Let's go for a walk." That meant that we would exit the yard by the back gate and head out toward the colored cemetery. Sometimes we would visit the graves of deceased family members and friends. Occasionally, we would get on the old railroad track and walk a mile or so until we saw a spot of forest Nannie wanted to explore up close. On the occasions when we found a chinquapin tree laden with nuts, we would take the time to pick a few of these tasty nuts before continuing our rather aimless ramble through the enchanting, multicolored forest. Eventually, Nannie would say, "It's time to head back." We would retrace our steps and return home with our spirits lifted by our leisurely stroll through the elegant trees and flowering plants that could be seen in great profusion around Southport in the fall of the year.

Like her mother, Mame, Nannie was not a regular at church. Perhaps this was because she earned such low wages that she did not have enough money after expenses to buy churchgoing clothes. After spending her money on nieces, nephews, and cousins, there was very little left. I would certainly rather see a sermon any day than hear one. Nannie's life was a sermon every day to those who paid attention. She did exactly as Christ commanded. She fed His sheep and helped clothe the naked. I feel sure that when she reached the pearly gates, St. Peter greeted her with a smile and said, "Well done, thy good and faithful servant." I look forward to seeing aunt Nannie again someday.

Not everyone in our family saw Aunt Nannie in the same light. In 2001, my first cousin Judy Gordon reminisced as follows:

I remember Nannie very well. She eventually got around to attending church every Sunday. [Judy's front-row seat in the St. James Church choir gave her a good view of the congregation.] I can see her in my mind's eye as she sat in her favorite spot in church – left side, second seat from the front, always in the space next to the aisle. Those who arrived after Nannie and wanted to sit on that pew would not dare ask her to move down so that they could get it. Instead, the latecomers would have to step across her. They would skip and hop until they were finally able to sit. It never occurred to Nannie to offer to move down to make it easier for the latecomers.

I remember repairing several outfits that Nannie used to wear. I used to take up anything that was too long or too big, and I would let out anything that was too little. She gave me a necklace that she had once worn to church. Though most of my siblings scattered when they saw her coming around Mrs. Shorty's corner, I never did try to avoid her that way. In fact, I never did let her complaining get to me. As I get older, I find myself becoming like her in some ways.

She used to fuss at Granny Mae [Judy's mother and Nannie's younger sister, Florence] as soon as she got in the door and sat down. If she didn't come around every day, she made it several times a week. Everybody agreed that Nannie was a complainer. But as I look back now, I don't think she was complaining; but rather, she was encouraging her nieces, nephews, and cousins in the only way she knew.

Nannie and Granny Mae were very different. I don't remember them talking to each other very much. Nannie would sit in her "spot" in the house. If you were sitting in her spot when she entered the room, you made it easy on yourself if you voluntarily moved. Anyway, Nannie would sit in her spot looking at the television, and Granny would sit in her chair with her legs crossed. She would swing the crossed leg while she watched television. Nannie was like me in that we could not stand the smell of Granny's cigarettes. I'm not sure if Granny put them out when Nannie entered the room or not. Nannie would twitch her nose like a rabbit. Jean [one of Judy's sisters] did that every once in a while. I would sometimes remind her that she was twitching her nose like Nannie.

Aunt Nannie tried to be a disciplinarian. I guess Aunt Nannie found out that she couldn't scare me with the cane she carried with her at all times. Eventually, she trusted me enough to allow me to fill out money orders for bill payments and deposit money in her bank account. I even completed forms for her Sears Roebuck catalogue orders. I remember a pair of gold hoop earrings that she got from one of the catalogues, but I'm not sure whether I placed the order. However, I do remember that I was the one who hung them onto her ears. She never allowed me to do anything for her without giving me fifty cents or so.

I don't think she knew anything other than work and church in her later years. Oftentimes, when trying to solicit money for her church board, she would say, "You'll pay it one way or the other." And I later accepted that rationale when giving my tithes and offerings. In fact, I learned much from being around her. I only wish she had laughed more.

I know Granny Mae [Judy's mother, Florence] must have loved her. When Nannie got sick, Granny always saw that either Bertha or I took her to the doctor. Later we went back and forth to the hospital for her leukemia treatments or for blood transfusions. Though she didn't live with Nannie, Granny washed her clothes and did all the things a sister would do.

When Granny died many years after her older sister, Nannie, she still had one or two items of clothing that had belonged to Nannie. She held on to these items as keepsakes to help her remember her older sister. I remember Nannie calling Cousin David's name with reverence. I didn't mean to go on so. I guess it's because of the death of my sister, Vermire. After a death in the family, we tend to look back on the lives of all that have gone on before.

Judy Gordon was Florence's daughter, and Florence was Grandma Mame's daughter. Consequently, Judy is my cousin.

Great-Grandpa Frank Gordon

Pa Frank, as Frank Gordon was called by all the grandchildren, was born in 1856 on a farm near Southport, North Carolina. The farm and

Pa Frank were owned by the Swain family. He was nine years old when he received his freedom from slavery. The late editor of the *State Port Pilot*, Jimmy Harper, published an article titled "Uncle Frank Gordon Teaches for Fifty-Five Years" on Wednesday, October 30, 1935. We learned much about Pa Frank from reading that article. But we were uncomfortable with the way our great-grandfather was addressed in the article. Jimmy Harper referred to him as "Uncle Frank Gordon," and Pa Frank was certainly not Jimmy Harper's uncle.

Mr. Frank (Pa Frank) Gordon
March 4, 1856-April 16, 1939

No white man in Southport in those days addressed any black man as "mister." If a white person wanted to show respect for a black woman or man, the appellations used were almost invariably "auntie" or "uncle." We also found it peculiar that Jimmy Harper referred to Pa Frank in a subheadline of that article as "good old darky." When you look past those bumps in the road, what you are left with is the only biographical sketch of our great-grandfather that was based almost entirely on what he said about himself. Harper felt that our great-grandfather was worthy of an interview because he completed fifty-five years of teaching and administration. Pa Frank told Jimmy Harper that he had taught more colored children in Brunswick County to read and write than anybody else, living or dead. Pa Frank retired in 1934 after teaching in one-room schools for over a half century. He was the first colored man in Brunswick County, North Carolina, to be appointed to the position of schoolteacher and later principal. Great-grandfather received his education mainly by attending a school in Southport which had been organized right after the Civil War by some white women in the community. The purpose of the school was to teach ex-slaves to read, write, and figure. His tenure in the school system ranged from the 1870s until he retired in 1934.

I taped an interview in 1979 about Pa Frank with my father's oldest sister, Eva Stratmon Lee. Aunt Eva Lee had been my seventh-grade homeroom teacher. She said that 'Fessor Gordon had been her first-grade teacher, and he was an excellent teacher. She further recalled that 'Fessor Gordon would make all the children line up against one side of the classroom, and one by one each student had to approach the teacher's desk. There, the student would sit on a backless wooden bench and recite for 'Fessor Gordon to prove that he or she had mastered the homework assignment. They would put a finger on *A, B,* or *C* and pronounce distinctly the sound for each letter. Then they would move on to new words such as *rat, cat, hat, tom, run,* and so on. After that, they would move on to simple sentences such as *Tom saw a rat* or *The cat ran after the rat.* Each student had to demonstrate that he or she had mastered everything in the primary reading book before moving on to a higher reader. Aunt Eva said that you were somebody when you finally moved from that primer to a higher-level reader.

All the students understood that they had to learn to pronounce, spell, and explain to the teacher what each word in the first book meant before progressing to the next level. She said that some students literally wore out the pages by pushing sweaty fingers along the lines nervously to show 'Fessor Gordon that they knew every word in that first book. In some cases, parents had to buy a second primer because pages were very worn out before some students had mastered all the necessary sections to 'Fessor Gordon's satisfaction.

All the children in school with Aunt Eva eventually mastered reading, writing, and arithmetic. There were no social promotions in 'Fessor Gordon's classes, and there were no failures. He worked with each student until each had mastered each level. As a result, his students all graduated and went into their rural communities where they were often the only ones around who knew how to read and write since this occurred just after the end of slavery. They became the leaders in their communities, and some of them became teachers. Some purchased land and became farmers. Students from this era insisted that their children learn to read, write, and compute. So what 'Fessor Gordon taught in little one-room schools had a tremendous impact on life in local colored communities for many years.

Aunt Eva Stratmon Lee also told me that my grandpa Frank was a noted speaker in the colored community. For instance, when the memorial services were held each May at the colored cemetery, 'Fessor Gordon knew how to weave local history and the Bible into a rousing speech that informed as well as inspired his audiences. The community choir which was directed by Mrs. Maude Howe would gather in the cemetery on May Day along with other musicians and speakers on the program. All the families would have cleaned and decorated the graves with flowers. Sometimes even a piano would be hauled out to the cemetery by a cart pulled by someone's mule, horse, or ox. The highlight of those occasions was Frank Gordon's inspiring speech. He always came through in a big way, according to Aunt Eva.

When he died in 1939, I was a fourteen-year-old ninth grader. I missed walking home from Sunday school with my much-revered and beloved Pa Frank. After his funeral, Great-grandma Nan told me that I could have his Sunday-go-to-meeting serge trousers. I was delighted since I had never had a pair of long pants before. Grandma Mame removed a pile of bedclothes and other items from the top of her foot-powered, fold-down Singer sewing machine. Then she nipped, tucked, and stitched until the trousers fit. I finally had my first pair of long pants. These pants were especially dear to me because they served as a memory-jogging keepsake that constantly reminded me of my beloved great-grandpa Frank. I regret that I never did ask him about his great-grandpa. Since Pa Frank was born only sixty-seven years after President George Washington took the oath of office as the first president of the United States, maybe I could have learned details about my family that might well have stretched back to the earliest days of the republic.

Great-Grandpa Miles Bryant

My paternal great-grandfather, Miles Bryant, was born a slave on the Lancaster Farm near Kinston, North Carolina, in 1853. Much of my memories of him come from my aunt, Eva.

Aunt Eva Stratmon Lee was a home demonstration agent for Brunswick County during the Depression in the 1930s. I used to accompany her on trips into the rural parts of the county where she helped farm families improve their canning skills. Usually by the time we arrived at a farm, the vegetables and fruits had been prepared and waiting for the canning process to begin. Aunt Eva would introduce whatever new techniques she had learned about how to can more effectively. After visiting several families, Aunt Eva would stop by Supply, North Carolina, to sit awhile with Grandpa Miles and Grandma Orilla Gore Bryant before returning to Southport.

During these short visits, I heard stories about how Grandpa Miles and Grandma Orilla Gore Bryant raised a family of eleven children. They had a farm that Grandpa Miles "stepped off" shortly after he was released from slavery in 1865 even though he was very young. He managed to raise tobacco and other cash crops. He also raised all kinds of fruits, vegetables, and farm animals. Whenever word got around that their cousin, Eva, was going to drop by for a visit, the members of the extended Bryant family would gather at the old homestead to share information. By the 1930s, when I participated in these visits, my great-grandparents were getting on in years; but they were still fond of chatting about the farm and various members of the family.

I learned that Grandpa Miles was somewhat of a manufacturer and a mailman. He used to make wooden barrels that he sold to people who were in the business of shipping turpentine from Brunswick County to factories far away. When the postman would try to deliver mail to hard-to-reach places along the rivers, creeks, and rough roads, Grandpa would help out. Grandpa would hook up his mule, Charlie, to a cart and help with the mail delivery, come hell or high water. At least, that is the way it was told to me. The pay probably was not much, but Grandpa considered it an honor to be the first colored man asked to deliver the U.S. mail in Brunswick County.

Grandpa helped to build the first colored school. Shortly after the end of slavery, he organized the colored men in the area, and they built a one-room schoolhouse. Then they petitioned the Brunswick County education officials to assign a schoolteacher to the colored community for six weeks of each year. If the Supply students wanted more schooling than six weeks each year, they had to walk seven miles down the road to Bolivia in order to attend school for the next six weeks.

Walking long distances was a small price to pay for some young people. The firstborn child of Miles and Orilla, Rhoda Bryant, walked daily the seven miles back and forth between Supply and Bolivia so that she could have twelve weeks of schooling each year. Rhoda became a teacher. She eventually married my grandfather, Joseph Stratmon, and they had six children: Eva Virginia; Charles; James William (Willie), my father; Lottie; Ophelia; and Josie. Aunt Ophelia, the youngest child of Rhoda and Joseph, died on December 29, 2005, in Houston, Texas, at the age of ninety-six years. She was born on February 9, 1908. A teacher for over forty years, she lived her life similar to her sisters Eva and Lottie. It seems that Grandpa Miles produced a family of achievers and hard workers. These stories about my grandfather and his family left me with a sense of awe at how they achieved so much under such a trying time in the history of our country.

As a matter of fact, these years include the Depression which meant that poverty was widespread among all races. Poverty accompanied by racially oppressive legislation, prejudice and hatred from the white community, unstable family structures, and psychological impediments resulting from an enslaved background are the type of ingredients which usually result in a low level of productivity. Yet many in this family seem to have gone against the tide.

Chapter 2

Post-High School Education

From a poor barefoot little boy playing around on the sandy roads of Southport to the hallowed halls of some of the best schools in the USA was an exciting and awesome journey. The schools are grouped together in this chapter, but as you will see, much happened in between going from one school to the next. I get back to those activities in other chapters. I will describe some of my feelings about my educational experiences here.

North Carolina Agricultural and Technical State University (NCA&T)

With the guidance of Grandma Mame, I came to the conclusion that if I worked hard and saved as much as possible, maybe by the second quarter which began in January 1942, I would have enough money to start college. If I could just get enough money to get enrolled, then maybe the personnel at North Carolina Agricultural and Technical State University (NCA&T) would help me find a part-time job. NCA&T had been established for colored students by the state legislature in 1891.

Grandma Mame suggested a strategy which was based on a plan used by her first son, Alison Gordon, who was the first member of our family to graduate from college. He had worked his way through NCA&T and had graduated in the 1930s. Mame figured that if her oldest son could do that without any monetary help from home, why not one of her grandchildren? The strategy worked. Though the registrar at NCA&T seemed surprised that I had the audacity to come to college with only $15 left in my pockets after I paid for a train ticket and college entrance fees, he decided to let me register anyway. He and I knew that I would need to find work immediately. With his help, I obtained employment at the A&P Economy Store in the produce section. As luck would have it, the store was within walking distance from the school.

That part-time job gave me the financial resources needed to remain in college, buy used textbooks, and take care of my personal needs without any financial help from home. I felt good about being able to make it on my own. I got down to the serious business of studying right away. Actually, I spent the lion's share of my time studying with the objective of making the honor roll. I succeeded.

After my first college semester was over, I went back to Southport and began to beat the bushes looking for a summer job. My cousin Charles Nelson McCoy was also a college student. He heard that construction companies in defense-related activities were hiring laborers in Norfolk, Virginia. Charles's roommate at NCA&T had invited him to come to Norfolk and stay at his house. I went along with him to check out the work possibilities.

Both of us found employment at the Barrett and Hipp Construction Company work site. The company was putting up around forty-five modular, frame houses each day, and I was taken on as a water boy. My job was to carry water in a bucket with a dipper to provide drinking water to the skilled workmen. They worked at a furious pace building low-income housing. The carpenters and plumbers were, of course, white. Only unskilled labor jobs were given to nonwhite laborers. I was glad to have any kind of job as long as it paid money that would enable me to return to college the following fall. The fact that discrimination was rampant in the company's hiring practices and pay policies was an unjust and mentally painful experience; I learned to live with it because I was so glad to have a job.

When the time arrived to return to Greensboro for the fall semester in September 1942, the USA was deeply involved in World War II. The emotional impact of the war played out on the NCA&T campus. Young male students were worried about the time when their call from the draft board would come. All of those who were at least eighteen years old might have to report for active service with the US Armed Forces.

I was worried too. As a kind of "ace in the hole," I took all of the Reserve Officer Training Courses (ROTC) that I could squeeze into my academic program. My plan was to earn a second lieutenant infantry commission upon graduation from college. But alas, that was not to be. Shortly after my eighteenth birthday on March 20, 1943, the draft board in Southport sent me a notice that I had been "selected by a committee of my neighbors" to serve in the US Army. I was to report to the Fort Bragg Induction Center at Fayetteville, North Carolina, on July 6, 1943. Practically every able-bodied male student in my class received similar draft notices, and we soon went off to war.

When our 3128 Quartermaster Service Company arrived back in the USA early in December 1945, we were told that the war in the Pacific was over. Because of this, our QM Service Company was no longer needed in the Pacific. We had heard about the atomic bombs that were dropped on Hiroshima and Nagasaki as we bounced from one wave to another on a US Liberty ship on our way home from the French port of LeHarve. By the time we landed in the USA, America had begun to disband the army that had been assembled to fight in Europe. Our company was discharged at Fort Meade on December 4, 1945. Each soldier was given an honorable discharge, a little pocket money, and a ticket home. This brings me to my decision to enter Howard.

Howard University

After visiting with relatives in Southport, I returned to NCA&T in Greensboro to resume my studies and to look after a few other matters. There was a beautiful young coed from Decatur, Illinois, with whom I had corresponded throughout my tour of active duty with the army. She had found someone else. Dejected and saddened, I decided that NCA&T was not the place for me to complete my bachelor's degree. I applied to and was accepted by Howard University in Washington, DC.

With funds made available to honorably discharged veterans under the terms of the GI Bill, I had almost enough money to pursue my education without the need for a part-time job. This financial freedom afforded me the time to spend many hours studying, and I did just that. I began my studies at Howard in January 1946. By adding on the credits I earned at NCA&T before being drafted into the army, I completed the requirements for the BA degree in commerce and finance by the spring of 1947.

Shortly after graduation, I reported to my new job at the Crown Savings Bank in Newport News, Virginia. Mr. Leroy Ridley, president of the bank, asked me to work as his personal assistant for a while before settling down to an assignment in one of the departments. I enjoyed the work. I probably would have made a career in banking had fate not willed it otherwise. I worked for the US Public Health Service in Monrovia, Liberia, after leaving the bank. I will return to this topic later.

University of Michigan

Near the end of my two-year tour of duty in Monrovia, Liberia, I decided that this was a good time to enter graduate school for further studies. This was in 1950, and I had completed two years with the US Public Health Service in Monrovia. I applied to and was accepted by the Horace Rackham School of Graduate Studies at the University of Michigan. My wife, Freddie Mae, was also accepted; and we made plans to take home leave after our tour of duty with the US Public Health Service Mission in Monrovia.

I also applied to the University of North Carolina at Chapel Hill. After some delay, the registrar's office telephoned me to say that I would not be allowed to enter that institution. However, if I wanted to go out of state and pursue graduate studies that were not offered by one of the colored state-supported colleges in North Carolina, the state of North Carolina would help pay the cost of my tuition. I was given the name of an official at the NCA&T in Greensboro whom I was to call on for further details about this program to help pay out-of-state tuition for "colored graduate students who wanted to study out of state."

I was approved. The state of North Carolina did in fact help pay my tuition for the four and one-half years that I attended graduate school at the University of Michigan. This was just one of the many instances of racial discrimination that all colored people seeking a higher education in those days had to endure. Since four of my great-grandparents had furnished free labor most of their lives as slaves in North Carolina, I felt that this tuition payment was some of the salary that was due my grandparents. I took the long-overdue money and focused on getting the additional education I needed.

Years later, when I was assigned to the American embassy in Paris, France, I received a call from one of my classmates from graduate-school days at Michigan who was then a full professor at the University of North Carolina. We had studied together and had earned the PhD in political science at the University of Michigan in 1955. He wanted to know if I was interested in teaching political science at the University of North Carolina. I declined his offer because I was very happy in my US Information Agency position in Paris.

After I retired from the US Foreign Service, I received another call from my fellow classmate and friend. He had become a division chair at the University of North Carolina, and he wanted to know if I had changed my mind about joining the faculty there as a member of the Department of Political Science. By that time, my wife and I were enjoying our work as faculty members at Rust College in Holly Springs, Mississippi. We had only recently built a new home as well; so we decided to stay in Holly Springs where we had finally settled after traveling all over Africa, the Middle East, and Europe.

Now, let me return to a discussion of the University of Michigan. When we arrived at the University of Michigan in the fall of 1950, we were assigned to houoing in Willow Run, about twenty milee from the main campus. That house in a low-cost public housing development was quite adequate, and we moved in on the day we arrived in Ann Arbor. Since many graduate students and their families were housed in the projects of Willow Run, the university regularly ran buses there from the main campus during the week and on football weekends. It was a very convenient arrangement.

All student families had to provide their own heating system. We also had to learn to cope with a wood-burning cook stove. Once we got settled in, my wife and I came to love Willow Run. We also relished the intellectual stimulation of graduate studies.

Freddie Mae and I searched for and found part-time jobs to help supplement our meager income. It was a shock to Freddie Mae to learn that the university had never hired any black females in secretarial positions. However, she broke that color barrier when the late Dr. Edmonson, dean of the School of Education, warmly welcomed her into his office. Freddie said that she felt like a member of the family of that hardworking administrative support staff. Once Freddie Mae completed her master's degree in vocational rehabilitation education, she continued her job as a part of the School of Education staff. In particular, she helped Dr. Edmonson complete revisions of his book on early childhood education. They remained friends until his untimely death. By that time we were living in a campus apartment in Ann Arbor, and I was completing work toward the PhD degree in political science.

When I entered the master's degree program in public administration in the fall of 1950, the Institute of Public Administration was headed by Dr. John Lederle. Dr. Ferrel Heady served as his deputy. Under their guidance, I began the grind of studying ferociously during the day and working at night to keep food on the table.

When I completed my master's degree in public administration in 1952, I was inducted into the Honor Society of Phi Kappa Phi because of the excellent grades I earned during those two years at the Rackham Graduate School. I went from a feeling of elation to a feeling of humiliation when I received responses to my job inquiries though. Neither cities inside Michigan nor outside Michigan were hiring African-Americans no matter how glowing were their resumes or how supportive were their references. On the other hand, every one of my white colleagues who graduated with a master of public administration degree in 1952 received interesting job offers. Public administration seemed like a hot job market if you were white, but not if you were African American.

I decided to remain at the university and work on a doctorate in political science. The passage of time has shown me that this was the correct decision. I found my studies fascinating and challenging. Delving into my studies helped to alleviate the pain of racial prejudice. By the winter of 1954, I had breezed through the required graduate courses, plus I had completed all of the required oral and written exams, including the stiff exams testing my ability to read French and German. I was overjoyed about my success on those examinations.

Thanks to a generous grant from the John Hay Whitney Foundation, I had spent six weeks in Monrovia, Liberia. The grant sponsored field research in order to fulfill the requirements for my doctoral dissertation on the US Public Health Service Mission in Monrovia. My doctoral committee chair, Dr. Ferrel Heady, arranged for me to defend my dissertation; and I was again boosted up emotionally when I succeeded. Dr. Heady told me to wait outside the conference room while the doctoral committee conferred. Relief came soon when Dr. Heady emerged from the conference room and addressed me as "Dr. Stratmon." At that moment, it seemed that a ton of weight had been suddenly lifted from my shoulders.

I hurried to the nearest telephone to inform Freddie Mae that we could now begin to plan the rest of our lives. Since a final copy of my dissertation was the only thing standing in the way of my doctorate degree, my wife and I decided to accept the standing job offer to teach at Prairie View A&M College in Prairie View, Texas. We agreed to go to Prairie View to take the teaching position, and I started work in January 1955.

My Greyhound bus trip from Ann Arbor to Prairie View was uneventful. Dr. T. R. Solomon met me at the bus station in Hempstead, Texas. Dr. Solomon had earned his PhD in political science in the University of Michigan in 1939, so we had quite a lot in common, and we became lifelong friends. He had even arranged for Mrs. Jimmie Fields to complete a final copy of my dissertation.

Dr. Solomon explained my duties and course load. He also told me that campus housing had been arranged for my family. We spent most of the time discussing US government contracts with Prairie View in which the purpose was to strengthen the Liberian school, Cuttington University College. Cuttington University College, located 120 miles north of Monrovia, is the oldest private, coeducational, four-year, degree-granting institution in sub-Saharan Africa. It was founded by the Episcopal Church in 1889. In light of my past experience in Liberia, I could understand why he wanted me at Prairie View.

After leaving Prairie View in 1956 to serve in the United States Information Agency, I attended the Foreign Service Institute which was held at the Arabic Language School in Beirut, Lebanon.

Arabic Language School

When my two-year tour of duty in Accra, Ghana, ended in 1958, my family and I arrived in the beautiful city of Beirut in February 1959. My mission there was to study Arabic. Prior to this trip, we returned to the USA to visit relatives in Gary, Indiana; Southport, North Carolina; and New Smyrna Beach, Florida. We wanted to reconnect with our roots, but also, we enjoyed visiting foreign lands and learning about different cultures.

Everything was so different from the world to which we were accustomed. The city of Beirut was often referred to as "the pearl of the Middle East." The smell of food was not like that of any other city we had visited. The smoked and spiced taste of the food was delicious. The people were very different as well. We were shocked when we saw so many men walking down the street sharing casual conversations and also holding hands as they strolled. We soon discovered that Lebanese males often walk about talking while casually holding hands. This in no way signified any kind of sexual orientation of either of the strollers. Also, we were amazed by the before-dawn call to prayer blaring from a recording atop the mosque which was near our house. We had never lived so close to a large Muslim community before.

We soon got to know many friends in both the Maronite Catholic Community and the various Islamic communities. It appeared to the casual observer that the Muslims vastly outnumbered the Christians. However, a political arrangement was worked out in 1949, in which it was declared as a matter of national policy that each religious group made up one-half of the total population. Once that decision was made, the two populations systematically divided up power. Half of the officers in the army came from each religious community. If the president was Christian, the prime minister had to be Muslim. If the admiral of the navy was Muslim, the army general had to be Christian, and so on. Of course, the Muslims had to work out agreements within their community about how power would be shared between the religious factions who lived under the general appellation of Muslim.

This power-sharing arrangement was placed in the National Compact, which was at that time given the respect accorded a national dogma that was beyond question in the media and other public forums. An objective observer might soon suspect though that the Muslim part of the Lebanese population was growing much faster than the Christians partly because Muslim men were allowed to have more than one wife and Christian men had only one wife. Consequently, many Muslim families had many children, while Christian families tended to consist of fewer children.

It had already been decided, however, that the population was half Christian and half Muslim, so there was really no need to stir up a hornet's nest by conducting a census. Besides, both sides agreed that the present arrangement was working, so why would they risk upsetting the applecart by conducting a national census. "If it ain't broke, don't fix it" seemed to be the prevailing philosophy in Lebanon at least between the years 1959 and 1961 when we were there.

I took pleasure in studying Arabic. My class spent about six hours daily in classes after which we would study at home for several hours each evening. Our manuals started with pattern sentences which covered topics about problems occurring in everyday life such as making introductions, ordering from a restaurant menu, holding casual conversations, and extending common courtesies. Once we had learned enough vocabulary, we spoke in Arabic throughout the six-hour day. We were encouraged to go into the local community to places such as restaurants, stores, and meeting places to seek out other instances in which we could use the language. After two months of study, we were required to spend a week with an Arab family. The family would then allow us to become immersed in the Arabic language by using it exclusively.

My week was spent with a family in the apple-farming region of Lebanon near the Israeli-Lebanese border. Besides the parents, there were ten children in that family, and other relatives lived nearby. They had been growing apples and other crops on the same relatively small piece of land for approximately five hundred years. They proudly explained that their family had been making a living on its small family farm long before Columbus discovered America. The whole family came out to greet me when I arrived late one afternoon in April 1959. They peppered me with questions about my family, my upbringing in North Carolina, my education, my African work, the Arab-Israeli dispute, and many other topics. We engaged in intense conversation until the evening meal of meat, vegetables, and bread.

On the next day, I accompanied two male family members on a shopping trip. As we shopped, they introduced me to many of their friends and colleagues. Later, we examined their farm. I can still remember how carefully they explained their cultivation methods as we walked through the rows of vegetables and fruit trees. They were able to produce enough food for the entire family. They did not need to buy anything but were able to survive independently. Each day, we walked about the farm, and they explained things such as how they protected the soil from erosion and how they knew each apple tree as if it were an old friend. They hoped that their family members would still be farming that small piece of farmland five hundred years hence.

When our discussions turned to politics, my hosts informed me that what they wanted most was to be left alone so that they could go on farming with no interference from the government in Beirut or from anywhere else. By the time my one-week visit was over, I had learned a new vocabulary in colloquial Arabic. Much of it pertained to the growing of apples and running a small farm in a rural setting. I doubted that I would be able to use much of this vocabulary in negotiations with foreign diplomats as we discussed international propaganda. So I realized that I had not mastered enough vocabulary, and I returned to Beirut rested but determined to study even harder than I had in the past, if that was possible. Typically, after six hours of study at the Arabic Language

School, I spent nearly four hours of study at home using tapes, reading Arabic newspapers with the help of my Arabic-English dictionary, and I occasionally listened to newscasts in Arabic on local television.

To increase my knowledge of the area, I also enrolled in two classes at the American University of Beirut. I had a wide choice of courses since many of the courses there were taught in English. I took two courses: the history of Islam and Middle Eastern politics and oil. My wife, Freddie Mae, like most other spouses, enrolled in Arabic study at the embassy. Our two sons had picked up quite a bit of Arabic by playing with local children. In addition, my wife and I took advantage of our location so close to the Holy Land to go to Jerusalem and other biblical cities during our holidays. Our two sons, Dave and Jimmy, went with us on these trips. They always seemed to enjoy themselves during our short visits to these historical towns and cities.

A curious event took place the first time we visited Jerusalem. We unpacked our bags and decided to go out and do a little sightseeing. Upon returning to the hotel, we found an elderly man with African appearance waiting for us outside the hotel. He said that he was from Jerusalem, and he wanted to invite us to his home to share the evening meal with his family. Out of curiosity, we decided to accept the invitation. He led us to a modest home located inside Hadrian's Gate where we met his wife and other members of his family.

When I tried to discuss Africa, our host seemed taken aback. He was not African. He was an Arab from Jerusalem, and so was his family for as far back as he knew. His wife had a very fair skin color, and their children were mainly light complexioned. He was curious about where we were from and how we happened to be in Jerusalem. Using our limited Arabic, we explained our circumstances, and we engaged in an interesting conversation. Then his wife and other female family members served a splendid meal. Before leaving we exchanged addresses, but we never did correspond. Even now, I wonder how they are fairing.

My next assignment came a few months before I completed the Arabic studies program. The personnel office in Washington informed me that my next assignment was going to be that of cultural attaché at the American embassy in Khartoum, Sudan, Africa. The Arabic Language School officials suggested that I devote at least an hour or so each day to learning Sudanese-Arabic, and I agreed. The US State Department Foreign Language Institute in Beirut found a graduate student from Khartoum who agreed to come to the American embassy several days each week to give me one hour of Sudanese-Arabic lessons. The school found Sudanese-Arabic books, tapes, and other materials; and I began to study. I found that this language was very different from the Eastern Mediterranean Arabic that I had already studied for a year and a half.

I did not go to Sudan as cultural affairs officer after completing my studies in Beirut. In anticipation of my arrival in Khartoum, my household effects were taken out of storage in Washington, DC and shipped to Khartoum, Sudan's capital city. Washington officials had not been informed that my orders were changed. I was instead assigned as assistant cultural affairs officer in Rabat, Morocco. I was shocked and disappointed, but I decided to put that behind me and soldier on.

My family and I went to Rabat, Morocco, and my effects went to Khartoum, Sudan. Our clothes and household effects sat in open-air storage in Khartoum for many months. When the US government sent my household effects from Khartoum to Rabat, what I received were boxes of useless, mildewed, and smelly fabrics. In spite of those misfortunes, I looked for ways to be effective in the new assignment.

I was never given an official reason why my assignment to Khartoum was so suddenly changed. However, I heard unofficially from an American journalist who was a frequent visitor to Khartoum that the American ambassador in Khartoum, who had a lovely swimming pool at his official residence to which he sometimes invited members of the embassy staff and their families for a swim, had vetoed the assignment of a black cultural attaché to his embassy. He probably feared that either he would have to invite me and my family for a swim or he would have to discontinue inviting other officers and their families. I have no official confirmation of these rumor-mill stories, but the sudden switch of my assignment looks suspicious even after the passage of decades.

National War College-National Defense University

The US Information Agency selected me to attend the National War College (NWC) for the 1970-71 academic years. The National War College, located in southeast Washington, DC, was renamed National Defense University a few years after I left. This decision followed my tour of service as director of the American Cultural Center in Amman, Jordan. I will discuss my term in Jordan later. All presentations and discussions at the NWC were classified. Because of this, I will not go into detail about what went on during my academic year there, except to say that it was a most rewarding intellectual experience, and the contacts I made there were helpful throughout the remainder of my career with the US Information Agency and the State Department.

However, the NWC played an important role in my journey from the small town of Southport to the world. Training missions of the Pennsylvania Air National Guard provided transportation for NWC students and faculty. We flew to Thailand, New Zealand, Australia, Japan, Indonesia, Pago Pago, and Korea. On some of these trips we flew over battlefields in which some class members had fought.

The courses were rigorous. In addition to the tough program of classified studies, each student was required to prepare an individual research paper. I spent the year researching the topic: "The Power to Declare War." The more deeply I delved into notes from the constitutional convention, leading constitutional law cases, and practices by Congress and the president, one thing in particular stood out. As I studied, the more certain I became that the founding fathers left us with a very flexible constitution; and that is, in no small way, one of the reasons the American constitution has stood the test of time so well.

Georgetown University Law Center

My tenure at Georgetown University Law Center extended from 1976 to 1980. So several years are in between, and those experiences will be detailed later. In short, I left Prairie View as a foreign service information officer with the US government. After spending two-year tours of duty in faraway places around the world, I returned to Washington and decided to go to law school.

I entered the evening school at Georgetown University Law Center in the fall of 1976. I had worked in various assignments in Washington, DC since returning from my last tour in Tunisia. The Office of Personnel at the US Information Agency (USIA) contacted me to state that they were in the process of working out my next overseas assignment which might be in Karachi, Pakistan. At that time, I had only one year left before earning the law degree, and I was not eager to leave Washington.

Therefore in 1979, when the USIA Office of Personnel advised me that Pakistan would be my next overseas assignment, I strongly considered retiring. The Office of Personnel notified me that I had accumulated twenty-nine and a half years of service. With information about my retirement options, Freddie Mae and I decided that it was time to retire from the foreign service. My retirement became effective on July 13, 1979.

I had fun studying law. The professors were all first rate, and every student was scholarly. Most of my classes at Georgetown were evening courses since I had a very busy day. After completing a full day at the US State Department where I was on detached duty from the US Information Agency, I would jump on my Kawasaki 1100 motorcycle and race over to the law school. That complete, I would hurry home through the quiet Washington streets.

After a quick snack of whatever I could find in the refrigerator, I would settle down to my daily grind of studying for the next night's classes. During the three and a half years that I was at Georgetown, I seldom got more than three or four hours of sleep. I was so exhilarated by the content of the courses that I hardly ever felt tired or sleepy.

Good times seldom last long; and after about two years of this demanding work and study schedule, my old nemesis, epilepsy, reappeared. I had been diagnosed with that malady in 1964 while on assignment in Fort Lamy, Chad. By the careful use of Dilantin and other medications prescribed by the medics at the US State Department and at the Bethesda Naval Medical Center, I thought that I had gained control of that debilitating disease and that it would not interfere with my work and school load. Eventually, it became obvious that I had only managed to cover up the symptoms. When law school requirements reduced my available hours of sleep to about three or four, I began to have seizures again. I also found that my memory was nowhere near what it was when I was a student at the University of Michigan graduate school nearly three decades earlier.

By the time I made this discovery, I had gone too far to drop out of law school, so I soldiered on. I managed to graduate from Georgetown University Law Center on February 1, 1980, a full semester ahead of my class. Unfortunately, after twenty-five years of epilepsy and with the loss of brain cells with each seizure, I was unable to pass the bar exam no matter how hard I studied or how many times I took it. Epilepsy had seriously degraded my ability to score high marks on the multistate portion of the exam. Fortunately, I had already begun receiving my pension from the State Department. Thus, I have mixed feelings about my stint in law school.

Chapter 3

US Army Service

My two years in the US Army got off to an inauspicious start. Although I have checked and referenced many of the details, some of my story is strictly as I remember it.

Induction

As scheduled, I reported to the Fort Bragg Induction Center on July 6, 1943. I was dismayed to find that my infantry ROTC training at A&T College in Greensboro, North Carolina, was going to be totally ignored. Although I scored high enough on the Army Intelligence Test to become an officer, I was told, rather bluntly, "All we have for you colored boys is work battalions." Work battalions meant that we weren't going to see combat action. I soon learned that this attitude was par for the course.

The racist hatred of white officers at the reception center at Fort Bragg toward minorities is unforgettable. I am overcome with somber emotions each year as June 6 nears and veterans gather to celebrate the D-day landings. On the other hand, if they had allowed me to train with and serve in the infantry, I probably would have been in the first few waves of fighting soldiers who waded ashore on June 6, 1944. No doubt, I would have been seriously wounded, killed, or captured. This was the fate of thousands of young white solders my age who were not shunted into relatively safe work battalions to serve behind American fighting troops. What a stigma! The army felt that black men were good laborers, but not good combat soldiers.

Wounded but unbowed, I continued to remind my quartermaster company officers that unlike many enlistees, I had scored high enough on the Army Intelligence Test to be sent to Officer Candidate School. My requests fell on deaf ears. I soldiered on as a quartermaster noncommissioned officer rather than as an officer in the infantry. These events, undoubtedly, shaped my destiny. It had not occurred to me that the good Lord may have decided that he wanted me to live and to do other work in His earthly vineyard before I appeared before His mighty bar.

Second Lieutenant David L. Stratmon, Infantry Reserved, 1947

We completed basic training at Fort Devens, Massachusetts. After that, we boarded a Liberty ship and sailed in a convoy of forty-two troop transport vessels to England. While there our company of about one hundred African-American soldiers was assigned for short periods to three friendly English towns – Needham Market, Stowmarket, and Ipswich by the Sea. For most of us, this was our first taste of life in which the white people we met did not seem to assume that we were inferior.

The Army Special Service Office arranged dances between my company and British girls. To say the least, we were as pleased as punch that the girls would show up to dance and socialize with us. Most of these guys were from Mississippi, Georgia, Tennessee, North Carolina, and South Carolina. A handful of the soldiers were from Washington, DC. Nearly all of us carried emotional scars resulting from living in a racist society.

All of the young men that I talked with felt a kind of sadness when it was time to move on. Several weeks after D-day, we left those friendly English towns and sailed for the Normandy coast of France.

3128 QM Service Company

Eventually, word came down to send some of the service companies to France. I found out that we were to give logistical support for the fighting troops. The 3128 QM Service Company rode over on American troop transport boats. I remember vividly that the boats ran right up on the sandy beaches at Normandy before we were ordered to disembark. Each man shouldered his duffle bag and his carbine rifle and waded through the knee-deep water onto dry land. We were in mainland Europe from 1944 to 1945.

The war brought heavy casualties. Our company had nothing but praise and a sense of awe for the infantry and marines who waded up those same beaches only a few weeks earlier. They charged on while facing blazing German machine gun fire, mortar, and death from other vicious German weapons. Of course, they paid a heavy price in injuries and casualties. Compared with what they did, ours was hardly more than a cakewalk up the beach. Our main worry was keeping our effects and rifles dry.

Our pattern of life in the war zone soon became routine. We were sent to this or that warehouse to load supplies onto army trucks. Red Ball Express was the way we referred to the trucks used to haul supplies from the beach and other stockpile areas near the front lines.

After handling ammunition and gas in France, Holland, and Belgium, the 3128 QM Service Company was sent to a small Belgium town called Froidthier located close to the German border. There, our orders were to bury American casualties. The soldiers' bodies were picked up each day from collection points near the front and hauled back in six-by-six army trucks. Our job was to open approximately one hundred grave sites each day and inter the soldiers. These casualties resulted from battles fought between the embedded German army and the First US Army which was commanded by General Hodges.

In the severe winter of 1944, the ground was frozen with several inches of ice with several inches of snow on top of that. That made the job of grave digging difficult. To say the least, it was really slow going with just shovels and pickaxes for digging. My job as a buck sergeant (three strips on my shirtsleeve) with about thirty soldiers under my command was to see that each man dug at least one grave and buried one of our fallen comrades. Nobody could leave the cemetery until the company quota of one grave per soldier had been met.

After completing our graveyard detail, we sometimes had to do other work. In addition to graveyard work, we often worked at a supply depot in the afternoon loading gas or other items needed up front by the fighting men. Once these jobs were finished, we could return to the abandoned Catholic school in Froidthier which served as our home during much of 1944 and 1945.

The American Battle Commission provided information about the current state of the cemeteries that we hastily prepared. According to the records of the American Graves Register Service of the quartermaster general, during WW II there were three temporary American military cemeteries established in Belgium. In an e-mail they sent to me dated December 16, 2004, the commission reported that following the war, all temporary American military cemeteries were disestablished. The remains were disinterred for repatriation to the United States for permanent interment in national or private cemeteries. Some were interred at the permanent Ardennes American Cemetery, at Neuville-en-Condroz, Belgium, or the Henri Chapelle American Cemetery at Henri Chapelle, Belgium.

The former temporary cemeteries were Foy U.S. Military that was located four miles north of Bastogne and established on February 4, 1945, and the Neuville-en-Condroz U.S. Military Cemetery located eight miles southwest of Liege and established on February 8, 1945. The

Henri Chapelle American Military Cemetery was located sixteen miles northeast of Liege and was established on September 28, 1944.

Melvin T. Bowman, one of my colleagues from North Carolina, was accidentally killed in 1944. He was buried in a temporary cemetery which we referred to as "Jay Hawk." Later, I learned that his body had been disinterred and moved to Henri Chapelle American Cemetery. This temporary cemetery which we called Jay Hawk was established near Henri Chapelle, Belgium, and that is where our 3128 QM Service Company was assigned in the fall of 1944. At the time of this writing, I could not definitively establish the exact location for the Jay Hawk Cemetery though. Research by the Museum December '44 failed to locate the cemetery as well. Returning to Belgium to solve this mystery is something I long to do.

We were issued new shoulder patches indicating that we were now a part of the First Army, whose commanding officer was General Hodges. I can never completely erase the image of the army trucks rolling into Jay Hawk with fifty or sixty of our combat dead, frozen stiff from the winter cold, piled like cordwood on each truck. Many of the soldiers who had fought and died in tanks came to us frozen in sitting positions. Unfortunately, we had no way to straighten their bodies without breaking their bones before burying them. We chose not to break any bones.

The grave registration team would check dog tags (metal identification tags worn by each soldier), prepare temporary grave markers, and note on their records the exact resting place for each soldier. There was no time for a burying ceremony or service. I do not recall seeing a minister or rabbi during the time our company worked in that forlorn burial place. We were there from the fall of 1944 until the end of the fighting in Europe when Germany finally surrendered on May 7, 1945.

Battle of the Bulge

During December 1944, the 3128 QM Service Company buried soldiers who had fought and died in or alongside the famous First Infantry Division. As the Christmas season approached, we were awakened one morning with the rumble of heavy artillery, and we noticed that the skies were pink from the heavy fire of big guns.

Later that day, we learned that General Gerd von Rundstedt, one of Germany's most illustrious senior military officers, had been given orders by Adolf Hitler to punch through the American lines and make a run for it to get as far as possible behind the American lines. For a while, it looked as though the Germans might succeed. The huge army trucks ran nonstop from the front lines back to Jay Hawk Cemetery to bring soldiers who had been killed in the Battle of the Bulge.

We were so busy trying to keep up with the increased flow of bodies from the front lines that we had little time to worry about our own safety. However, we couldn't ignore the pounding of the German divisions and the return fire by American and Allied forces which continued around the clock.

General George Patton, commander of the American Third Army; General Courtney Hodges, commander of the American First Army, to which our unit was attached; and British general Bernard Montgomery soon put together a counterattacking force that took the wind out of the sails of General Gerd von Rundstedt. He was first stopped, then rolled back to end the last significant German attempt to break through the noose that the Allied forces were tightening. With the Allied forces advancing from the west and the Russian juggernaut rolling into Germany from the east, slowly the enemy was weakening.

Soon there were fewer bodies to bury. Our company was transferred to towns and cities in West Germany where we helped supply manual labor at warehouses, fuel and ammunition dumps, and other supply points during the spring of 1945. These duties helped pass the time as we waited for orders which eventually came to move to LeHarve Harbor in France where we could board ships to return home. When we boarded ships at LeHarve, we were scheduled to undergo additional training in America in preparation for assignment in the Pacific Ocean. It seemed that everyone assumed that the Japanese would fight to the death when American forces tried to invade their final bastion, Japan.

Several of my colleagues in the 3128 QM Service Company were not anxious to leave Germany. The beautiful girls in every village, hillside, and city were so gracious that leaving was hard. Although fraternizing with Germans was against orders, it was hard for those young men to resist when they were far from home. The temptation was especially great when we were stationed in large cities such as Dusseldorf, Aachen, and Essen. All of these cities were bombed by Allied forces and then nearly destroyed by our artillery fire during the final push by the Allies from the French beaches to the heartland of West Germany.

The beautiful young German girls treated us like celebrities. They were waiting for us at each city. They were well versed in the fine art of negotiating and bartering. Most of the goods at stake were cigarettes and chocolate. These items could be exchanged for services of equal value. The amount of time spent bargaining and the value of the goods and services was a matter up for negotiation.

Somehow, negotiating seemed easy for non-English-speaking girls and our soldiers, none of whom spoke German or French. One of our comrades from Mississippi confided to us that he might desert when the time came to leave Germany. He said that he was considering staying in Germany because he had never seen such friendly women back home in Mississippi. However, when the time came to leave, he looked sad; but he made no effort to carry out his threat to remain behind. Like everyone else, he took his seat on the train and waited patiently for four days for an engine to arrive to pull the train to LeHarve Harbor. I guess many of the men had mixed emotions, but I can't recall anyone who wasn't looking forward to boarding that Liberty ship for the trip home.

PART II

Chapter 4

Monrovia, Liberia

After serving during World War II from 1944 to 1945, I returned home, finished college, and accepted a position in a bank in Newport News, Virginia. But I didn't stay there long because I worked in Monrovia from 1948 to 1950. This chapter covers my activities while in Monrovia.

Administrative Assistant

From out of the blue, I received a call from Mr. John Eason, liaison officer for the U.S. Public Health Service Mission in Monrovia, Liberia, West Africa (USPHSIML). He explained that a vacancy for someone with my training in business administration had occurred in the USPHSIML. He wanted to know if I was interested in being considered for the position of administrative assistant to the Liberian mission. He said he had spoken to Professor H. Naylor Fitzhugh, my faculty advisor at Howard University, and he recommended me for the job.

Mr. Eason and I had several telephone conversations. He mailed packages of documentation to me which I eagerly studied. Within a few days, I accepted his offer, and I was hired for the job.

I went to Washington for briefing by US Public Health Service officials. The officials there arranged meetings with diplomats at the Liberian embassy and other people who formerly served in Liberia. I also read several books describing the country and its people.

I called my Howard University classmate and sweetheart, Ms. Freddie Mae Anderson, of Gary, Indiana, to advise her of my good fortune. I told her that I would be leaving the USA early in January 1948 to fly to Africa to take up my new post. Freddie Mae's response was "When are you going to send the ring?" I was taken aback! There had been no talk about a ring before, but she perceived that if I flew off into the wild blue yonder, I might find other interests, and our long courtship at Howard would come to naught.

Mrs. Freddie Mae Stratmon

I went to Newport News, Virginia, after I completed requirements to become a civilian employee of the US Public Health Service. The Crown Savings Bank of Newport News was where I had been working as an assistant to the president, Leroy Ridley. There, I gave notice to President Ridley and all my friends that I was leaving to accept a job in Liberia.

I also went to a jewelry store in Newport News and purchased an engagement ring for my girlfriend. She and I decided to tie the knot immediately. Some of our friends in Washington, especially Catherine and Wilbert Smith, helped us find temporary lodgings in Washington and a Methodist minister in Rockville, Maryland.

Catherine Smith and I had been classmates at NCA&T College during the 1942-43 school years. Wilbert Smith and I had served for two years in the 3128 QM Service Company of the US Army during World War II. With their help, everything went well. Freddie and I rushed through the wedding and honeymoon. Then Freddie Mae returned to Gary, Indiana, while I flew off to West Africa. A few weeks later, Freddie Mae traveled aboard a Farrell Line freighter to join me in Monrovia. That long and happy marriage lasted for just over fifty years – from January 15, 1948, until Freddie Mae's death on March 3, 1998, in Holly Springs, Mississippi, after a prolonged illness.

Brief Description of Liberia

Liberia is a small West African country, bordered by Guinea, Ivory Coast, and Sierra Leone. With a total land area of 1,585 km, it is slightly larger than the state of Tennessee.

As of July 2004, Liberia's population was estimated to be 3,390,635, with an average life expectancy of 48.15 years. The literacy rate for those fifteen years or older was 57.5 percent in 2003. Approximately 40 percent of the population is Christians, 40 percent have indigenous beliefs, and 20 percent are Muslins. The estimated HIV/AIDS rate was 9 percent. Approximately 74 percent of the workforce was employed in agriculture. Annual per capita purchasing power was estimated to be about $1,000, and around 80 percent of the population lived below the poverty line in 2001.

When some plantation owners in the United States began to include in their wills that favored slaves would be freed upon the death of the plantation owner, the abundance of freed slaves soon became a problem. The American Colonization Society was created to deal with the people who had formerly been slaves. That organization sent explorers to West Africa to find and purchase land which could be used by these freed men and women.

The US government commissioned a merchant ship, *Elizabeth*, to transport eighty-nine freed people from New York to West Africa in 1820. At first, they settled in Sierra Leone. In 1822, American naval vessels helped transfer the settlers from Sierra Leone to what is now known as Liberia.

By July 26, 1847, only twenty-five years after the first freed people from America landed in what is now Liberia, that country declared itself to be an independent nation. Though the threat was ever present that British or French colonies would try to take land, Liberia remained free and independent. The centenary celebration in 1947 was a very happy event for the country, especially for the Americo-Liberians, as the descendants of the former American slaves called themselves.

US Public Health Mission

The US Public Health Mission in Monrovia grew out of a small group of medical personnel who were sent to Liberia in 1944 by the US Public Health Service. Their purpose was to protect the interests of American and Allied powers in and around Roberts Field. An advance team of a medical director, an engineer, and three or four other officers prepared the groundwork for the health mission. Additional personnel arrived later.

My flight from New York to Liberia in January 1948 was uneventful and long. The major airlines were still using propeller-driven planes in the 1940s for transatlantic flights. After a change of planes in Dakar, Senegal, West Africa, we flew down the west coast of Africa to Roberts Field which was located approximately sixty miles from the capital city of Monrovia. The large airfield had been used by American and Allied military aircraft during World War II. They were on lookout for German U-boats that were attempting to interrupt South Atlantic shipping during World War II.

Although the airfield was large enough to accommodate large propeller-driven aircraft, it was in many ways primitive. For example, when a plane approached at night, workmen would run out and light lanterns that were placed along the runway. That weak source of light helped guide incoming planes to safe landings at Roberts Field.

When the war in Europe ended in 1945, the health mission continued to exist but with a different focus than it had originally. The American government would help Liberia improve its very limited health services. Particular attention was to be paid to environmental sanitation, malaria control, and training of paraprofessional medical personnel. Some people were trained to spray insecticides regularly on the interior walls of every house and every pool of standing water in the Monrovia area. This would help with mosquito control.

The health mission's compound was always a beehive of activity. We mainly used the school system to spread the message that Liberians could reduce the morbidity rate drastically by following our recommendations. They needed to increase environmental sanitation, boil drinking water, and make sure that all school-age children were taken to the health clinics to get free shots and medications which could control whooping cough, measles, diphtheria, smallpox, ulcerated sores, and other health problems. Laborers had to be paid their weekly wages, and supplies needed for construction of a paraprofessional nursing school had to be purchased. We constructed an entire health compound. The staff and engineers were kept busy with these various tasks. The health clinics were open as much as eleven hours a day to treat the enormous number of clients. Sometimes the waiting lines stretched into nearby streets.

The Liberian government, under President William V. S. Tubman, was completely supportive of our efforts to eradicate preventable diseases. For example, when some homeowners refused entry to our malaria control teams, President Tubman ordered that all houses must be opened to the malaria control teams so that they could spray insecticides as part of the mosquito-control program. The research data that we collected showed that there was a steady decline in infant mortality, a significant reduction in malaria, and an improvement in the environment. Thus, the health mission was deemed successful in health education, malaria control, and preventive health care measures.

By 1951, the health mission had worked itself out of a job. Liberians had gradually taken control of most of the operations. They supervised the daily operation of the health clinics, the malaria-control program, the health-education efforts, as well as the training of laboratory assistants and paraprofessional medical personnel. To speed up the transfer of the mission to the Liberian government, the Liberian Public Health Program was physically transferred into the US health compound.

When the Liberian people were ready to take over public health, the US officials merged what remained of the former health mission with a US economic mission. This group had been sent to Liberia earlier to help with economic development of that country. The US Public Health Service personnel remaining in Liberia thereafter turned their attention toward helping to form a public health program in up-country Liberia.

This program demonstrated how the American government could approach health assistance and other AID programs in developing countries. The US Public Health Service did, in fact, send US Public Health Service commissioned officers into nine other countries after the Liberian mission experience. During the early 1950s, the US Public Health Service assigned commissioned personnel to technical assistance missions that had public health and sanitation components in Egypt, Ethiopia, Libya, Iran, Iraq, Israel, Jordan, Lebanon, and Saudi Arabia.

Chapter 5

United Nations Family

In between traveling and taking on various assignments, we collected children. This was a labor of love. We adopted four children from different parts of the world: Liberia, USA, Switzerland, and Tunisia. Two stepchildren were added when I married Lillian Jean.

Monrovia, Liberia – Laurice

Our United Nations-type family began in Liberia and just grew. After my family and I had been in Monrovia for almost a year, a Liberian woman whose name was Annie Watson approached Freddie Mae and asked her if we would take her little girl back to America when we returned home. She said that she had a baby by a Lebanese merchant when she was barely a teenager, and the little girl was now living in Kakata, Liberia, about an hour outside of Monrovia. She said that her sister had made arrangements to send her baby boy, Butch, back to the USA to become a part of the family of Nurse Mary Lee Mills. Nurse Mills was the most senior registered nurse with a commission in the US Public Health Service among the officers who were assigned to the health service mission in Liberia.

Freddie Mae and Nurse Mills put their heads together. Before we knew what hit us, Annie had gone to Kakata and returned with her daughter, Laurice Jamil Sadd. She wanted Laurice to move in with us immediately so that there would be no last-minute hitch when it was time for my family to leave Liberia. Freddie Mae's aunt, Gladys Williams, suggested that we send Laurice to her in Gary, Indiana, so that she could enroll her in the Catholic school which was located just down the street from her house. When we returned to the USA in 1950, we adopted Laurice, and she became the first of our four adopted children.

At the time of this writing, Laurice lives in Washington, DC. Married three times, she is the mother of three intelligent children. Sonya, Laurice's oldest child, and her husband have adopted beautiful twins who were just short of their first birthday when they became a part of our family. Paul and David Henry are her other two children.

San Antonio, Texas – David Jr.

When I went to Prairie View A&M University in 1954, Freddie Mae and I decided to adopt another child. This time, we got in touch with the Texas Cradle Society. The society asked us to come to San Antonio to adopt a twelve-day-old African-American boy. We made that youngster a part of our family in 1955 and named him David Jr.

Glarus, Switzerland – James

When I was assigned to the American embassy in Beirut, Lebanon, during the years 1959-1961, my wife and I started to look around for yet another addition to our family. This time, the UNICEF, the organization that concerns itself with children and their welfare, advised us that it was holding an eighteen-month-old Jewish boy in Glarus, Switzerland, who understood the German language, but no other. He was up for adoption. Freddie and I had studied German while in college but made no claim to any fluency in that language.

Freddie Mae made arrangements to fly up to Switzerland to pick up the child. Jimmy, as we called the third addition to our family, who was born to an unwed Jewish girl in Glarus, Switzerland, soon fitted in nicely with our growing family. We named him James Dunlap Stratmon, with James being the name of my father and older brother who are both deceased. His middle name of "Dunlap" is the family name of Freddie Mae's maternal grandmother. Freddie Mae's mother died when she was only two years old.

Jimmy now lives in Durham, North Carolina, with his wife, Edwina, and their daughter, Jessica Louise, who entered NCA&T University at Greensboro as a freshman in September 2007. Jessica's grandparents in Switzerland would, no doubt, be happy to meet her. I hope they can get together someday.

Tunis, Tunisia – Wassila

I was on assignment at the American embassy in Tunis, Tunisia, North Africa, when we adopted our fourth child in 1974. Freddie Mae had become a volunteer at the Kasir Said Orphanage near Carthage, Tunisia, which was the ancient capital of the Roman Empire. Tunisia became capital of the western part of the Roman Empire after the fall of Rome in AD 410. Freddie Mae raced her battered French sedan up the hill to our house in Gammarth, Tunisia, one day and excitedly announced that a couple from California had come to the orphanage and wanted to adopt "our baby."

The baby she was referring to was a one-year-old girl from the Bedouin tribes of southern Tunisia. The orphanage staff had given her the name of Merriem. Freddie insisted that we must go quickly and file papers on Baby Merriem so that she would not be taken to California. Almost before I knew what happened, we found ourselves at the Kasir Said Orphanage with the necessary papers in hand and with a little Bedouin girl smiling at us.

The lady in charge of the Kasir Said Orphanage asked what we were going to name Baby Merriem. I happened to look up at one of the walls in the reception room at the orphanage and saw a large photo of President Habib Bourguiba's wife, Wassila, staring at me. I said we will name her Wassila Merriem Bourguiba Stratmon. Freddie Mae said Wassila Merriem was okay but that "Bourguiba" added on to that was too much, so she became Wassila Merriem Stratmon.

Wassila attended CADET Catholic School and Holly Springs High School, followed by four years at Rust College from which she graduated with a BA degree in social work in 1995. She is now working as a social worker for the District of Columbia. She is married and has two children: Demi Sahara and Drew Amani. Wassila's husband, Dwan Jordan, is an assistant principal during regular session and serves as a principal during the summer sessions in the Washington, DC School System. He received A grades at Shaw College in Raleigh, North Carolina, and at Trinity College in Washington, DC.

Evanston, Illinois – Lorenzo

Lorenzo Guerrero was born in 1961 in Evanston, Illinois, and he is my stepson. After attending St. Paul's Grade School and St. Augustine High School, he graduated from the University of New Orleans with a bachelor's degree and a double major in economics and English. Besides traveling in Israel, Europe, and Africa, he has held the position of investment banker with Stuart James Investments. After leaving the banking field, he became a teacher trainer for eighteen-wheel truck drivers.

New Orleans, Louisiana – Jeanne

My stepdaughter, Jeanne Guerrero, was born in 1968 and attended grade school at the Ursuline Academy in New Orleans and graduated with honors from the North High School in Atlanta, Georgia. She received her bachelor's degree in journalism from Louisiana State University where she was on the dean's list and also received a scholarship from the *New York Times*. After graduation she joined the public relations team of the mayor of New Orleans.

Jeanne earned a master's degree from the Delta State University. Following that, she became a technology specialist with the Southeastern Regional Vision for Education (SERVE). Later, she was appointed executive director of TheCommunity@Emain in Louisville, Kentucky, before moving on to become the director of Technology and Community Development at the University of Louisville.

Jeanne's accomplishments earned her a place in *Who's Who International.* Her four-year marriage to a Georgia Tech trained engineer, Darrell Moore, ended in divorce. She has one daughter, Savannah, from that marriage.

Chapter 6

Prairie View, Texas

Prairie View A&M University, the first state-supported university in Texas for African Americans, was established in 1876 during the Reconstruction period after the Civil War. I was employed there as an assistant administrator in the Office of the Dean and as a professor of political science from 1954 to 1956.

Prairie View A&M University

In 1945, the name of the institution was changed from Prairie View Normal and Industrial College to Prairie View University, and the school was authorized to offer, "as need arises," all courses offered at the University of Texas. In 1947, the Texas legislature changed the name to Prairie View A&M College of Texas. On August 27, 1973, the name of the institution was changed to Prairie View A&M University, and its status as an independent unit of the Texas A&M University System was confirmed.

Dr. T. R. Solomon was the academic dean at Prairie View during my tenure there. He was a remarkable college administrator, and I was delighted to be asked to work in his office as assistant administrator of the Prairie View-Liberia Project. I also served as a professor of political science in the Department of Political Science. Since I had just come away from four and one-half years of intensive graduate study at Michigan, I was delighted to get into a classroom in order to challenge and encourage young African-American students. This was an especially appealing time in history right after the US Supreme Court ruling in the *Brown v. Board of Education* case in 1954.

Dr. Solomon was one of the first African Americans to earn the PhD in political science from the University of Michigan. The degree was conferred on him in Ann Arbor in 1939. By the time I left the University of Michigan in the winter of 1954, he had been employed at Prairie View for a number of years as professor of political science. When I was employed there, he was head of the Prairie View-Liberia Contract. He was also the advisor to President E. B. Evans.

Dr. Solomon was trying to find personnel to go to Liberia to convert Cuttington College into an agricultural and technical college similar to what Prairie View A&M University had been for nearly a hundred years. Cuttington College was established by the Episcopal Church of America on February 22, 1889. Financing for the Prairie View-Liberia Project was provided by the US government through the US Agency for International Development (USAID).

I was asked to help recruit faculty members to go to Liberia for the purpose of working at Cuttington College. I soon found that it was a real challenge to work the telephones trying to find faculty members with engineering and other technical qualifications who were ready to pack up and go off to Liberia for a year or two. But finally, the call of exciting adventure in West Africa in a challenging academic environment was appealing enough to attract the faculty we needed.

Gold Coast, West Africa, Job Offer

My wife and I enjoyed living in Texas so much that we began to search for a lot to build our dream house or a house to buy so that we could remain there for many years. However, that was not to be. Hardly a year had passed, before I started to receive calls from Washington inquiring with regard to whether I would be interested in a career in the US Foreign Service. At first, my response to these overtures was that I had spent over a year overseas with the army during World War II and an additional two years in Liberia with the US Public Health Service Mission in Monrovia, Liberia, and I was not interested in going overseas again soon. Therefore, I was now looking forward to putting down roots and building a home for my family in Prairie View.

The State Department was not impressed. They put pressure on me by using the name of Dr. Jim Pollock, dean of the Department of Political Science at the University of Michigan. He had told them that I would be a good candidate to become a US Foreign Service officer. They assured me that my first assignment was likely to be on the staff of the US ambassador at the United Nations in New York. Concurrent with these discussions, calls came from the US Information Agency (USIA) Office of Personnel to find out if I was interested in a career appointment with the USIA. Eventually, I advised the USIA that if they could find a job for me that would enable me to be in the Gold Coast when it achieved its independence from Great Britain in 1957, I would accept their offer to offer to join their overseas staff.

The agency informed me that a group of examiners from the USIA would be in Houston, Texas, the next month to interview applicants for employment. The interviews were held at the Jesse Jones Hotel. Everybody at Prairie View knew that the Jesse Jones Hotel in Houston did not allow African Americans to even use the front door and certainly would not allow me to be interviewed in their facilities alongside white applicants. When I informed the USIA of this, they made light of my assertion that the hotel was known to have a well-publicized racist policy. Subsequently, the USIA asked me to meet the panel of examiners in a conference room at the hotel.

Early on the appointed day, I arrived at the hotel in downtown Houston. I went straight to the front desk to say that I had an appointment with the panel of examiners who represented the USIA. A clerk summoned up years of race hatred and rudeness to utter the phrase, "This hotel does not allow colored people to use the elevator." I used the telephone though, and I called the panel of examiners to give them the news. I waited to see what would happen. Shortly, two examiners came to the front desk to escort me to the elevator. Alarmed, the desk clerk urged us not to use the elevator but to take the stairs. We walked up four flights.

When we reached the fourth floor, we learned that the clerk had sent someone to the fourth floor to insist that African Americans not be interviewed in the same room as whites. No mixing of the races was allowed. The hotel volunteered to hang a sheet across one end of the fourth floor and equip that little hideaway with a table and chairs. The examiners interviewed me about my credentials and qualifications while sequestered behind that sheet.

The officers were so embarrassed that they could hardly focus on the predetermined questions. After we struggled through that humbling experience, the officers apologized profusely for putting me through that kind of treatment.

My job offer from the US Information Agency came a few weeks later. My first assignment was to be cultural affairs officer at the US consulate in Accra, Gold Coast, West Africa. Freddie Mae and I were overjoyed. Suffering through the terrible experience at the Jesse Jones Hotel in Houston had paid off.

We said farewells to our many friends at Prairie View A&M and took our two children, Laurice and David, and went to Washington for briefing in preparation for the new assignment in West Africa. When all necessary training and medical procedures were complete, we were put on a transatlantic flight for London. After a short layover, we changed planes for the long air trip from England to the Gold Coast.

Chapter 7

Accra, Ghana

It was an exciting time to be in the Gold Coast. The Gold Coast became known as Ghana after receiving independence from Great Britain in 1957. Everyone we met was talking about the great day of independence that was at hand when we arrived in that beautiful British colony in the fall of 1956.

Independence Day

The British governor general, Sir Charles Noble Arden-Clarke, had conveyed official assurance to Prime Minister Kwame Nkrumah and the parliament that Her Majesty's government would turn over power in the Gold Coast to Prime Minister Nkrumah and the parliament on March 6, 1957. So the struggle by the Convention People's Party and other groups had almost reached a happy outcome for the people of the Gold Coast and England just a few months before I arrived in Accra.

Leading up to that day, the city was abuzz with activities. In fact, the city of Accra had insufficient hotel space to accommodate the throngs who would come to help celebrate independence. I was among the official greeting party when Vice President Richard Nixon arrived for the celebrations. However, Mr. Nixon's accommodations were arranged by the US government before he arrived.

Vice President Richard Nixon (left) and Dr. David Stratmon
in Accra, Ghana, airport as he arrives to represent the USA
at the Independence Day celebrations in March 1957

Expecting overflow crowds, the government of Ghana asked anyone with an extra room in which visitors could stay to register with the Office of Tourism. Since we had an extra room, we registered.

Late one night, we were awakened by the loud knocking of a guide from the Office of Tourism. He wanted to know whether we still had the room to let. If so, Mr. and Mrs. Lester B. Granger from New York wanted to occupy it. We were honored to have the executive vice president of the National Urban League and his wife, Lefty, share our modest home.

Our conversation with the distinguished couple lasted for nearly an hour before we escorted them to our spare room which we had furnished with a locally made bed and mattress. That mattress felt like it had been made from corn shucks. It definitely was not the most comfortable mattress in the world, but any port in a storm. We watched closely as Lefty and Lester came downstairs the next morning. We could see that the mattress had been unkind. Gracious people that they were, they laughed it off and thanked us over and over for putting them up. They stayed with us for a week. The Grangers were charming guests, and we were glad that we had signed up to take in strangers who had arrived in the Gold Coast and found that there was no room at the inn.

The Independence Day celebration was a grand affair. People from all over the countryside converged on the capital city and filled the streets. As far as the eye could see, people were shoulder to shoulder and wall to wall. We observed many revelers with tear-filled eyes. Excitement was in the air. The main event was held in a large square where the national parliament was housed. After much dancing, singing, and speech making, the British flag was lowered at the stroke of midnight; and the flag of the new nation, Ghana, was raised for the first time in public. The new national anthem of Ghana was played by a military band, and everybody waited with much pent-up emotion the arrival of the admired and celebrated man of the hour, Prime Minister Kwame Nkrumah.

While awaiting Dr. Nkrumah's arrival, I looked around at the dense crowd in front of the parliament building and noted that almost everyone assembled there had tears of joy streaming from their eyes. Not many people will ever have the privilege of being present at the birth of a new nation. Freddie Mae and I agreed that Ghana's independence was the most exciting event we had ever witnessed.

Dr. and Mrs. Martin Luther King Jr.

The Ghanaian government made every effort to have a successful celebration. When a friend at the Ministry of Information noticed that Dr. Martin Luther King and his wife, Coretta, were sitting in the Ambassador Hotel lobby looking bored, they asked me to come over to the hotel to check on them. My wife and I had arranged a dinner for some of our Ghanaian friends from the Ministry of Information and from the Ministry of Education, so we asked the Kings to join us. In fact, I drove over to invite them in person. They accepted my invitation. They took a taxi to our home later that afternoon.

Dr. King and Mrs. King seemed to enjoy meeting the young Gold Coast leaders and our guests. They participated in a lively and interesting conversation. After our Gold Coast guests left, the women went to the living room to talk. Dr. King and I retired to my front porch, pulled off our shoes, put our feet up on the banister, and talked casually until late that afternoon. Our conversation covered topics such as civil rights, the Montgomery bus boycott, racism in America, and the growing independence movement in Africa. The memory of that discussion will always be with me. I published an article for my fraternity journal in which I reviewed that visit.

When Dr. King told me about threats he had received against him and his family, I asked if he had considered moving away from the South as a precaution. Without hesitation, he told me emphatically that he was aware of the danger, but he was going to continue his work to make America a better place for all without regard to skin color. It was evident that he was prepared to pay any price required to achieve his goal of helping to wipe out racism in America. I was deeply impressed with this dedicated servant of God.

I drove the Kings back to their hotel at around sundown, and I did not see them again, except on television.

Cultural Affairs Officer

My job as cultural affairs officer was to use all of my energy and available resources to inform the people and the leaders of the Gold Coast about American life and culture. We have achieved wonders in the United States, starting from thirteen struggling colonies that, like the people of the Gold Coast, had to go through a bitter campaign before the colonial power, Great Britain, agreed to let the American people rule themselves. I tried in every way I could to show that the American free market system was vastly superior to the methods of economic life chosen by Russia, China and others. I wanted them to use the American model as their pattern for structuring their own free-market system and the democratic political system whose legitimacy should be based on the consent of the governed.

In order to sell these ideas about the American way of life, we used many approaches. Some of them were the Fulbright-Hayes Educational Exchange Program, visits to the Gold Coast by American scholars and artists, scholarships for a few outstanding Gold Coast students to study in America, and close contact with the in-country media to make certain that the American side of every political story was brought to the attention of all editors. In addition, we operated a first-class library with books about all aspects of life in America.

Dr. David Stratmon sharing books about life
in the USA with Ghanaian civilians

From time to time, we received traveling art exhibits about life in America that visited all large cities in Ghana and some important smaller towns and villages. We organized a speaker's bureau that could supply speakers covering a wide range of topics for any group that wanted an American speaker. The five or six American officers who staffed the US Information Agency office in Accra just before the Gold Coast became the free country of Ghana were constantly seeking opportunities to meet with students and teachers at the high schools and in colleges to inform them of our American way of life.

Cultural Attractions

Dr. Kwame Nkrumah, the first president of the new country, gave an audience to American high hurdler, Jack Davis, when he visited Ghana shortly after Independence Day. Jack Davis put on a public demonstration of his amazing speed and agility in high-hurdle jumping. He ran circles around the local athletes all of whom seemed to be having a good time as they ran around the track behind Jack Davis. As an ambassador of goodwill, Jack Davis was right at home. He mixed easily with all audiences including his brief visit with President Nkrumah and senior officials from the Ministry of Youth and Sports. This visit was public diplomacy at its best.

Ministry of Youth and Sports official (left), Dr. David Stratmon, President Kwame Nkrumah, Olympic Gold Medalist Jack Davis, met with two other Ministry of Youth and Sports officials in Accra, Ghana, in 1957

We were aware that the Russians were very actively engaged in a well-funded propaganda campaign designed to make all of the new nations nearing free statehood status in Africa adopt the communist political and economic systems. Our job was to make certain that the new nation of Ghana, the first of these newly independent African nations south of the Sahara, would not decide to follow the Russian model. Our traveling exhibits and visiting American musical groups were always well received especially in up-country towns and cities where exposure to the American way of life had been limited.

Music was always an attractive propaganda tool. The Wilbur de Paris New Orleans Jazz Band first gave concerts in Accra, after which

I escorted them to Kumasi and to the Trans-Volta Togoland region of Ghana. The band was accorded the red-carpet welcome everywhere they put on a concert including Kumasi which is the home of the Ashanti tribe.

A village elder in the small city of Ho in the Trans-Volta Togoland region listened attentively to the jazz concert and then approached me with this question: "Where do you think that kind of music originated?" He listened to my explanation about how the music began in New Orleans and worked its way up the Mississippi River to Chicago and then spread from there to New York and to the rest of America and to the world. He responded that that was not quite the true history of this kind of music. This kind of music, the elderly Ghanaian said, had begun where the small town of Ho is located; and it had been played there for many generations. He said he was overjoyed to see and hear that the music from his village and tribe had taken root and was thriving in America.

Ghana-America Society

Our Ghana-America Society, which I helped organize, drew together all Ghanaians and their spouses who had studied in American colleges and universities. We tried to meet at least once a month for a meal and conversation. If a young man or woman expressed an interest in studying in America, we could always call on a member of that group to help counsel and advise the student(s) who wanted to continue their education in an American school. I believe that our attempts to strengthen the ties of friendship that existed between Ghana and

America were successful. Too soon, it was time to leave this historic country.

Many of our Ghanaian friends came to the airport to see us off when it was time to leave that beautiful and exciting country. My wife and I were sorry to see our tour come to an end, but the two-year assignment was finished. In those days, rotation routinely occurred for Americans working in the US Foreign Service after a two-year tour of duty. We were delighted to receive notice, however, that my next assignment was a two-year stay in Beirut, Lebanon.

I was assigned to the US State Department's Foreign Service Institute to study the Arabic language in Beirut, Lebanon, for two years. I studied Arabic from February 1959 to February 1961. I also engaged in area studies with a focus on such hot-button issues as petroleum, religion, and the Israeli-Palestinian problem.

Chapter 8

Rabat, Morocco

Following my studies in Lebanon, I was assigned to the position of assistant cultural affairs officer in Rabat, Morocco. My family and I were there between the years 1961 and 1963.

By the early 1960s, the Cold War was in full stride, even in Morocco. We tried to get to know as many of the governmental leaders as we possibly could. Our mission was to help them understand that an open, free society like America was in tune with what young graduates of the University of Morocco should want for their country.

Communism

Russia was using all possible avenues to win over the hearts and minds of Moroccans. We tried to counter Russian propaganda by disseminating propaganda of our own. Our Voice of America (VOA), with its powerful transmitters along the West African coast, was beaming information about our society across North and West Africa twenty-four hours a day seven days a week in English, French, and Arabic.

We did our best to make sure that all media including newspapers, television, and radio were given accurate and up-to-date information. We supplied copies in Arabic of all official statements about Morocco and the Middle East made by our president, leaders of the Congress, the secretary of state, and other top American government officials. We constantly added to the American Cultural Center collection of books about America that were available in English, Arabic, and French. We made available loads of film clips, feature stories, and other information to radio and television stations located throughout the country. Through the use of branch cultural centers in Casablanca, Tangiers, Marrakesh, and Fez, we made certain that our side of the story was being hand-delivered to important media and cultural leaders by our officers posted in those Moroccan cities.

Use of the Fulbright-Hayes Educational Exchange Program was especially effective. It gave us the wherewithal to send leaders and students to study in America. As students, they could see what our open and free society was like. In many cases, we were able to help Moroccan teachers, engineers, and other professionals earn advanced degrees in America. These students had to agree to return to Morocco when they completed their studies and use their American education to help build a better society in their homeland.

Cultural Attractions

In addition, the Fulbright program made it possible for us to bring the best of American culture to Rabat and to small up-country cities. For example, when the Family Blue Grass Band from Berea, Kentucky, was sent to Morocco, we arranged for them to play and tell the American story in an open-air concert held in Rabat in an ancient Roman amphitheater. We strung lights and arranged other amenities. We were delighted that on a beautiful moonlit night, invited officials including the following: cabinet ministers, teachers, students, political leaders, tribal leaders, newspaper representatives, and electronic media moguls along with many others, enjoyed American bluegrass music in a Roman amphitheater. As well, we sponsored a tour which included the band in addition to other cultural attractions. They traveled to up-country cities where they were equally effective in telling the American story to Moroccans.

We enjoyed our work and the opportunity to explore different countries and cultures. It was exciting to be able to arrange for a Moroccan polyphonic string ensemble with handmade musical instruments to visit America. They played their beautiful Moroccan music for selected audiences in several cities scattered across the United States. None of this group, except for the tour guide, spoke any English, and none had ever been outside Morocco. They returned from the tour very pleased with the reception given to them by Americans. Several immediately enrolled in our free English classes.

The Cuban missile crisis was a crisis for some, but it was an opportunity for us. It allowed us to use our resources to show that our version of how the world had come to that crisis was more believable than the "claptrap" they were receiving from Moscow. Fortunately, we had already cultivated the contacts needed to deliver our message. Consequently, we were able to achieve our goal of undercutting the untruths being spread by the Russians.

Chapter 9

Fort Lamy, Chad

After serving tours of duty in Ghana, Lebanon, and Morocco, I was assigned to the American embassy located in Fort Lamy, Chad. N'Djamena is the capital city of Chad now. Lying in southwestern Chad in the confluence of the Chari and Logone rivers, the city was formerly known as Fort Lamy. It was Fort Lamy when I was there, so please bear with me if I continue to call it by that name. Neighboring countries are Niger, Libya, the Sudan, the Central African Republic, Cameroon, and Nigeria. I served there as director of the American Cultural Center and embassy attaché between the years 1963 and 1964.

On Arrival

When I flew out of the national airport located just outside Washington, DC in Alexandria, Virginia, headed for my new assignment in Fort Lamy, it was winter in Washington. When we arrived in the capital city, the weather was anything but winter. The heat was stifling, and we had to contend with sand as well. As one travels to the north in Chad, gradually, plant life disappears; and at the northern border the immense Sahara Desert takes over. If any wind is blowing from the north toward Chad, the sand from the desert becomes a strong environmental factor to contend with. The temperature would sometimes reach 120 degrees Fahrenheit during the middle of the day, and sometimes it reached 100 degrees at midnight. I soon got used to it.

Some locals adapted their office hours to accommodate the heat. The old-timers told new arrivals that you had to arrive at the office by 7:00 a.m. and beat a retreat to your living quarters at noon. There you would relax until the midday heat lifted at around 3:00 or 4:00 p.m. "Only British and mad dogs stirred about during the noonday heat," old-timers liked to remind newcomers.

One of the first problems I had to deal with was education. My two young sons, David and Jimmy, needed to be in school. My wife and I were informed by friends at the embassy that the only school for boys six and eight years of age was run by the French Catholic sisters. We visited the school to see what could be done.

During the interview, the head of the school told us, "Bring the two boys over and leave them. They will pick up French in a hurry." She was absolutely right. Within a few weeks, they were running around the house playing games they had learned at school, and they were using the French language. Perhaps this was because they did not know English words that could be used in playing their new games. They quickly became bilingual. Of course, the fact that they also lived after that in French-speaking Kinshasa, Congo; Paris, France; and Tunis, Tunisia, provided them with the opportunity to become fluent during their youth. Consequently, the language has remained with them.

Director of Cultural Center

I was cordially received by Ambassador Brewster Morris and his wife, Mrs. Ellen Morris. The ambassador reviewed the political and economic situation in Chad for me in great detail. We discussed my role as a part of the embassy team and my service as director of the American Cultural Center. My staff and I were expected to help strengthen the cultural and educational ties between Chad and America. At this time, the two countries were experiencing good relations.

We were given first-class office space for our work in downtown Fort Lamy. The staff consisted of three American officers and fourteen Chadians. Each employee seemed dedicated and well trained. Our Cultural Affairs Section of the American Cultural Center was in charge of the Fulbright Program. Through this program we were able to arrange for a limited number of Chadian leaders to visit America to interact with professionals in their work specialties. We also had funds to send a few Chadian students and young leaders to America each year for short-term study.

Only a few Chadians spoke and read English well enough to undertake degree-related study in America in the early 1960s. We did, however, have a very well-attended spoken English teaching center in Fort Lamy, which was open to Chadian students and government officials alike. Many students stayed with the program until they acquired enough English to feel comfortable in any English-speaking social setting. Some progressed to the point of conducting business in English with their English-speaking contacts.

We had the best library in town. There were hundreds of books in English and French which were aimed at high school-level youngsters. When the French granted independence to Chad in 1960, they left only one secondary school in the entire country, and that educational institution was located in the southern part of the country in Fort Lamy. The principal and several of the teachers were French, but they seemed to welcome our donations of books and other materials about the United States.

Dr. David Stratmon helps some young students access
resources in the American Cultural Center library
in Fort Lamy, Chad

Our press section at the American Cultural Center was always headed by an American foreign service information officer. The press section head maintained close ties with officials at the Chad Ministry of Information and supplied them with official texts of policy statements of the executive and legislative branches of the American government. We worked hard to ensure that all policy statements by American senior political leaders about Africa, the Middle East, and Asia were placed in the hands of key officials in the Foreign Ministry, the Ministry of Information, and the president's office as soon as we received them via our overnight wireless file.

When we received the latest official text of policy statements hot from our wireless file, we translated them into French and rushed them to local contacts. Sometimes we met our Russian counterparts either going into or coming out of these Chadian offices. In 1964 when I arrived, Chad had not yet developed a television service. However, there was a radio station there which could be heard in all of the major towns. Because we needed access to this transmission service, we cultivated good relations with the Chadian Ministry of Information officials who ran the radio station.

Cultural Attraction

Washington sent a notice to us that the All-American Brass Band from New York City had agreed to make a tour of West Africa under the sponsorship of the US Information Agency. Immediately, we requested that the band be scheduled for a three-day visit to Chad. When the schedule was finally complete, four days had been included for Chad.

Ambassador Brewster Morris informed President Francois Tombalbaye of the plans for the tour and asked for his assistance. The president obliged. He ordered lieutenants in the Ministry of Interior and in the Ministry of Cultural Affairs to enlist every drummer group in Chad for participation in a welcoming ceremony to be held in the capital city. Soon, the streets of Fort Lamy were crowded with musicians, especially drummers, from almost every town of any size.

The main event for the American drummers was held in the Fort Lamy soccer stadium. That soccer stadium was nowhere near large enough to seat the hundreds of musicians from all parts of the country who had either hiked or caught a ride on the back of trucks. The decibel level within the city reached a high pitch as the drummers tried to outdo each other as they rehearsed in the streets and parks along the way to the stadium. On the day the event was scheduled, dignitaries, including President Tombalbaye, members of the Chadian cabinet, the diplomatic corps, students from the secondary school, the football teams, wives, girlfriends, family members of VIPs, and everyone else came to the stadium.

The Chadian musicians and drummers performed first, followed by the All-American Brass Band from New York City. The result of this contest of bands should have been foreseen, but it was not. When the drummers from all over Chad walked, danced, and pranced into the stadium, the sound was unbelievably loud yet rhythmical. The crowd went wild. The noisy entrance by the Chadian musicians was a hard act for anybody to follow; however, the All-American Brass Band gave it their best shot. They came into the stadium playing American marching band songs with as much gusto as they could muster. That was not enough. The Chadians didn't scream and jump for the Americans as they had already done for the homeboys. On the other hand, their appreciation was sincere.

Chadians, from the president down to the lowest student sitting in the bleachers, felt grateful to the American embassy for bringing this group of professional musicians from New York to Fort Lamy. This allowed the Chadians to feel good about the fact that although Chad did not yet have tall buildings and other modern conveniences, Chad definitely had musicians, especially drummers, who could hold their own against professional musicians from any part of the world. Such was the feedback following the tour which included Chad and other parts of Africa.

Up-country

Ambassador Brewster Morris was determined to visit every major village in this landlocked country in north central Africa. The total population of Chad is slightly larger than the city of New York, and many of the regions were difficult to reach, and facilities were not modern. The ambassador and I visited major villages that were accessible by roads.

Occasionally, Ambassador Morris would notify me that he planned to visit this or that up-country town or village and that he wanted me to accompany him and bring along a generator and a projector so that we could show some films about America to the paramount chiefs, their advisors, and other guests. The term "paramount" refers to a chief who is over several villages. We would typically prepare to leave a small collection of books in English and French with someone designated by the chief. If a school existed, we would leave books and supplies there.

One village about one hundred miles north of Fort Lamy stands out in my memory. There was no school, and we wanted to know why. Other local officials along the route to this village had built schools. We inquired of the chief why he had not started the process of sun-baking mud bricks for the purpose of building a school so that the young people in his town could get some education. His response shocked us. He said, "Only one person in this village can read and write, and that person works for me as my interpreter." Clearly, this paramount chief knew that knowledge is power. Since he could not read himself, he was determined not to let things get out of hand by having a lot of youngsters in his village become literate.

Ambassador Brewster Morris (left) and Dr. David Stratmon
(right) present gifts to representatives of the village chiefs of
Chad from the American People-to-People Committee

Following our conversation though, the chief promised to open a reading center in his village. He graciously accepted our gift of books and other materials. The chief was more enthusiastic about the gift of volleyballs which the ambassador offered as a token of the friendship that existed between the American and Chadian people. The volleyballs had been sent to the ambassador by the People-to-People Committee in the USA who asked that they be distributed to youngsters as he saw fit. All Chadian young people played soccer, but hardly any knew how to play volleyball. No doubt, the new volleyballs served just fine as soccer balls.

Epilepsy

After about eighteen months in Chad, I was suddenly knocked off my feet. I had epilepsy! I had heard of the disease, but since no one in my family, as far as I was aware, had ever had epilepsy, I was blindsided by this serious condition. When I suddenly lost consciousness one night, Freddie Mae and Dr. Vanpoole, the embassy regional medic, rushed me to the hospital in Fort Lamy. They learned that not only did I have a seizure, but also I had broken my right collarbone in the process. Upon rethinking their decision about the hospital, they believed it would be better to fly me up to an American army base hospital in Germany for examination and treatment.

After a bit of rest and recuperation for my family and me in Germany, the USIA decided it would be best for me to return home and enter the Bethesda Naval Hospital. When I returned to Washington shortly after the first seizure occurred, the doctors at the US Department of State medical facility determined that I had suffered an epileptic seizure and immediately put me on a regime of medicine. I was cautioned to take the medicine daily for the rest of my life. "You lose brain cells every time you have an epileptic episode," they warned. In those times, no one knew that epilepsy is sometimes caused by tapeworms which can enter the body through unclean food. Severe seizures can follow. We had purchased almost all our food at the local market where sellers had no refrigeration for freshly slaughtered meat products; water to clean vegetables and prepare them for market were almost certainly contaminated with many kinds of harmful bacteria and animal life, including tapeworms. Merely washing and cooking products from Chadian open-air markets posed serious health hazards. I am still an epileptic, but at the age of eighty-two, I am in reasonably good health.

The doctors at the Bethesda Naval Hospital carefully examined me, paying special attention to the broken collarbone. I wanted to know if I would gain full use of my right arm without an operation. The surgeon at the naval hospital put it humorously. He said that since I could "wash my face and wipe my behind," they were not inclined to operate. Never again was I able to raise my right arm above my head, but I seemed to be okay, and I became well enough to return to normal duty.

I was worried; and I wondered if my career in the US Foreign Service, which I had found to be promising and rewarding, had come to an abrupt end at the young age of forty. I had enjoyed the work until I became ill in 1964. Fortunately for me and thanks for the warm support of Freddie Mae, my career in the foreign service did not end. Her positive outlook on life was infectious and left no room for depression, so I soldiered on.

During the next fifteen years after I was diagnosed as an epileptic, I served in very responsible positions in Washington, Paris, and Tunis. However, it became increasingly apparent that after I became an epileptic, I had lost a part of whatever it was that promotion panels were seeking. It is safe to say that epilepsy caused me to request early retirement at the age of fifty-four in 1979. I had spent twenty-nine and a half years in federal service and with fifteen years after my first epileptic seizure in 1964.

I can fully understand and sympathize with the father of the epileptic described in the New Testament who stopped Jesus on the side of the Mount of Transfiguration and begged Him to heal his son who was an epileptic. Jesus healed the young man and reminded James, John, and Peter that they had been unsuccessful in their efforts to heal the epileptic because of their unbelief and lack of faith (Matthew 17:14-21). I refer to this biblical quotation because it reminds me of three things: first, that epilepsy is an ancient disease; second, that suffering by those who have the disease can be redemptive; and third, that by maintaining a strong faith in God, the suffering will not be in vain.

Chapter 10

Washington, DC

Back in Washington, I served as desk officer in the Africa division of the USIA between the years 1964 and 1967. The desk officer worked as a liaison between the USIA headquarters in Washington and branch offices in various countries around the world. I had already served in four of the countries: Ghana, Chad, Congo, and Liberia. So I was pleased that these were among the countries assigned to me for oversight.

Desk Officer

I quickly settled in and read mountains of correspondence which passed between the eight countries assigned to me and the USIA in Washington. I decided that I could be most useful by trying to improve the backup support that the USIA was providing its overseas posts. With that in mind, I visited and got to know the people running the Voice of America (VOA), a powerful radio system that blanketed the world with programs in most of the major languages. These programs were much more important than mere headline news about America. Indeed, the VOA beamed all kinds of programming to its worldwide audiences, including educational, political, social, and other topics too numerous to list here.

My travels and work in other countries gave me insight into how many of the programs were used. I knew that in West Africa the programs broadcast in a slowed-down version of English, called "special English" by the VOA staff, were very popular for a variety of reasons. One particular reason was that teachers and their students used the broadcasts to help improve their command of the English language. Gaining information about the American way of life was an added advantage of listening to these programs.

I made myself available to the USIA film section. They regularly sent documentaries and other filmed material to our overseas cultural centers for placement with media outlets or to be added to the collection of films in the loan libraries of the American Cultural Centers in different countries. Producing new film was one of the activities of the film section. They asked me to go to New York to preview some of their filmed pieces about life in America that were still in production and intended for placement on African TV stations. The producers of these documentaries seemed pleased to have input during the production stage of filming from someone who had lived in some of the countries.

I reacquainted myself with other components of the Washington USIA. The hardworking USIA professionals in our Washington press section and the exhibits section were among my contacts, and they constantly turned out materials that they felt would help explain American culture. Our overseas posts needed documents they produced which could explain our political and economic system or which could tell how this land of immigrants had managed to become unified enough to develop from a band of thirteen British colonies along the eastern seaboard into the world's strongest economic and military power.

Before I was assigned overseas, I had made orientation visits to all of these USIA Washington media production facilities. I knew that they were in the business of providing field posts with films, books, exhibits, press releases, and other resources. Field posts then used these materials in their daily work abroad in order to inform audiences about this wonderful country. Now that I had actually served on the other end of this chain of American propaganda, in the good sense, I took a greater interest in what these USIA Washington elements were including in their films, books, pamphlets, and exhibits. I also took careful note of their wireless file output and what the Voice of America was beaming to the rest of the world.

I was pleased that my first assignment in Washington allowed me to get to know the personnel who worked in these parts of the USIA.

Associate Director of the National Museum of African Art

From 1975 to 1976, I served as associate director of the National Museum of African Art which followed my assignment in Tunisia.

Mark Lewis, director of the African division of the USIA, called me one day and asked me to drop by his office. He told me that the National Museum of African Art had asked that a USIA Foreign Service information officer, with recent service in Africa, be placed at the museum on loan for a year. The National Museum of African Art had been started in southeastern Washington near the US Supreme Court building by Warren Roberts, a former USIA officer. Mark Lewis asked me to go over and talk to Warren Roberts, the founder and director, to see if something could be worked out.

I was surprised to find that the National Museum of African Art, though operating on a shoestring, owned seven brick townhouses which were acquired by Warren Roberts. We decided that I would serve there for one year. When I arrived at the museum to begin working, Warren Roberts informed me that the collection of African art at that time consisted of around of five thousand wooden statues, artifacts, ceremonial masks, and other priceless pieces of African art. The place was a beehive of activity, with school buses lined up in the streets almost every day of the week to transport children from Virginia, Maryland, and Washington schools to take escorted tours.

Some of the tour guides were Africans who knew firsthand experience how the African masks and other art objects had been used in rites of passage and other ceremonies in western, central, and eastern Africa. The many questions that the students and other visitors asked after their tours indicated to me that they were learning a lot about Africa through the study of art. Many returned with their friends as the museum continually changed the exhibits.

Muhammad Ali at the National Museum of African Art

When I heard that Muhammad Ali was going to be in the Washington area, I contacted Mrs. Evelyn Ligons, Freddie Mae's cousin, who sometimes traveled with the Ali party. I wanted to know if the champion could be persuaded to visit the museum since he was in the area preparing for his upcoming fight against challenger Jimmy Young.

I decided to drive out to the Ali camp in nearby Landover, Maryland, to hand-deliver an invitation from Warren Roberts to Mr. Ali requesting that he visit the museum.

I was surprised by the air of informality that pervaded the training camp of the champion of the world. I was especially surprised to see so many attractive young ladies milling around. I asked a male member of the entourage why there were so many pretty girls at the training camp. He explained that the champ "knocks out three or four pretty young girls most mornings." He said the young girls chosen for this exercise on a given morning were lined up in separate rooms, and the champ would visit each one. Until today, I do not know if the young follower of Muhammad Ali was simply spinning a yawn or if he was telling the plain truth. On the other hand, the women were there. He may have made up the some of it when he told me that part of the champ's preparation for a fight was to have rapid-fire romantic encounters with many pretty young girls.

When he visited the museum, Mr. Ali and his party arrived in a couple of limousines at the appointed time, and we gave him a tour of the collection. After the tour, Warren Roberts asked the champ if he had any comments. The champ looked around and said, "I don't like nothing but pretty art." This was obviously not his kind of art. We were shocked, but we had to admire his frankness. Although Muhammad Ali won that fifteen-round fight and retained his world heavyweight championship title, some of his trainers believed that he did not knock the opponent out because he took time out to visit the National Museum of African Art on the day before the fight and had, therefore, lost his usual three-day period of concentration. They did not provide an explanation of the value to the fight of the young women who were around close to fight night. They said that the champ always "psyched himself up" during the final three days before a fight, and generally he did not allow anything to intrude on his three-day mental preparation. Thus, Ali's visit to the museum was the reason that the fight had dragged on for fifteen rounds. This visit by the renowned boxing champ probably was not a big winner for the museum.

Smithsonian Connection

Prior to my arrival on assignment to the museum as the associate director, Director Warren Roberts and his staff had started a campaign to make the National Museum of African Art a component of the Smithsonian Institution. If that could be achieved, the future of the museum and the collections it held would be better protected, and the exhibits could be viewed in improved displays. During one of the strategy meetings, we decided that Mr. Roberts should call upon his long friendship with Senator and Mrs. Hubert Humphrey for help. He would ask the senator to introduce a resolution in the US Senate and in the US House to call for the Smithsonian Institution to become the new home of the National Museum of African Art. To help move this project forward, the museum staff arranged to visit every senator and congressman to urge congressional support for the resolution.

We needed to improve our chances for success, so we invited Senator and Mrs. Humphrey, Secretary of State Henry Kissinger, and many other notable public officials to make visits to the museum. At the request of Warren Roberts, I visited a number of African American officials in the greater Washington area to ask for their support for our efforts. Sometimes I was met with only lukewarm support, and sometimes I was met with skepticism. Apparently, a group of African American leaders had failed in an earlier attempt to get an African art museum placed on the mall similar to the one already built there for the display of Far Eastern art. Since that effort had not succeeded, some African Americans seemed unenthusiastic about Warren Roberts, a white man, succeeding where they had failed.

Eventually, the National Museum of African Art became a part of the Smithsonian Institution. When that happened, Warren Roberts was given a high-level special appointment and an office at the Smithsonian. He deserved recognition because of the fact that he had spent his personal fortune and many years of his life putting together such a magnificent collection of African art. It was clear, however, that some Smithsonian officials felt that Mr. Roberts's usefulness was at an end; they preferred that he step aside and let them run the show from then on. Step aside is what he did.

Many people in the community were not satisfied with the outcome. Some African American community leaders complained that when the Smithsonian finally decided to open a museum of African art, they buried the whole thing beneath the ground on the mall. Nonetheless, the National Museum of African Art is a magnificent belowground structure containing outstanding displays which provide world-class insight into African culture. I am proud that it is a part of my history.

Chapter 11

Kinshasa, Congo

After spending two years at the National Museum of African Art, it was time for me to end my appointment and undertake another overseas tour of duty. Agency personnel advised me that an opening was available as information officer in Kinshasa, Congo, and unless I had serious objections, that would be my next assignment.

Information Officer

I began immediately to prepare my family for the exciting new assignment in the Congo. We undertook a long list of preparations, and the following is only part of what we did: made arrangements for shipping our furniture and household effects, found someone to care for our Alsatian-German shepherd dog which we brought all the way from Chad, prepared the car for shipment, informed my two small sons that they would need to make new friends in another French-speaking school, and read post reports informing us of what special items to consider purchasing. Some things would not be available in this developing country located in the heart of Africa.

At last, a big commercial jet airliner landed us at the Kinshasa airport. The usual welcoming team from the administrative office of the embassy was waiting to help us through customs and take us to temporary living quarters in downtown Kinshasa. They told us that we would be safe there since our apartment was on the sixth floor of a modern hotel and presumably safe from robbers.

We enrolled the boys in school and, with the aid of the embassy administrative section, searched for suitable living quarters. Since several of the families in the embassy and the USIA had nice houses with swimming pools, we decided to look around to see if we could find a house with a pool. I left these household details up to my very capable and experienced wife, Freddie Mae, and the helpful staff of the embassy administrative section while I turned my attention to my new position as information officer for the post. My office was located in the American Cultural Center, and it was there that my American colleagues and embassy officials put me through the usual itinerary of briefings.

I began to make the rounds of the media officials in the government of the Congo which included radio, television, and print media. There was no free press in the Congo in 1968; but such as it was, I called on the leadership and made known my availability to help them with information about the American system of government, including information about our Congress, our presidential system, our state and local governments, the federal court system, and so on. In addition, I offered them the use of the wealth of documentary materials about the American way of life available in French and English at our American Cultural Center.

I began to follow up on these initial contacts by personally delivering texts of official statements by senior American government officials about political and economic matters that we routinely received over our wireless overnight file from Washington.

Israeli Kibbutzim

During our short assignment in Kinshasa, we got to know several members of the Israeli embassy mission and saw them often on the social circuit. Israel had sent seasoned kibbutz builders to the Congo for the purpose of increasing self-sufficiency in food production by establishing farm cooperatives up-country that would be modeled after the successful kibbutzim that the Israelis had built in modern Israel. President Mobutu and his cabinet approved the idea of sending some of the unemployed young Congolese into the rural towns and villages to work on the farm. At the same time, they would strike a blow at the large concentration of unemployed young people who were idle and being drawn into antisocial activities in the large city of Kinshasa.

The Israelis complained that as soon as they rounded up a group of young people and persuaded them to go up-country to work on farms, the young people would slip away from the farms and catch the first thing rolling or hike back to the lights of the city and the antisocial activities that they had given up in order to farm. The government seemed unable to force these young people to give up city life for the rigorous life on a farm. The Congo had the potential to become the breadbasket for African countries below the Sahara since it had adequate land and water to become immensely productive in the agricultural sector. But that was not to be at that time; however, new developments along these lines have in recent years overshadowed the failures of the past.

Chinese Agricultural Aid Mission

While we were in the Congo in 1968, an agricultural aid mission from mainland China was hard at work, but they were not helping the Congolese people. President Mobutu had the entire mission working on his private farm and gardens in Kinshasa. There was a lot of smirking during socials in and around Kinshasa about the reports sent back to China about the effectiveness of their agricultural team. If their mission was meant to curry favor with General Mobutu, they were successful; but if they were sent to the Congo to help the Congolese people in general, then they had very limited success since their physical and human resources were so completely devoted to working the gardens and farms of General Mobutu. Unfortunately, there has been little evidence that this type of administrative mismanagement has changed throughout the years.

Chapter 12

Amman, Jordan

On the day my car arrived in the Congo from America, I received notice that I was being transferred to Amman, Jordan. We were stationed in Amman between 1968 and 1970.

Director of American Cultural Center

My new position would be director of the American Cultural Center in Amman. USIA personnel had recommended me for this important position because the records indicated that I spoke, read, and wrote Arabic. The person occupying the position in Amman had become ill and was being returned to Washington for medical attention. While I looked forward to this challenging assignment, it would mean that our children would attend three different schools in a single year. I was just getting to know my way around the bureaucracy of the Congolese government, but orders are orders, so we packed our bags and flew off to Jordan. Besides, our travels were especially sad because we had just received news of the assassination of Dr. Martin Luther King in Memphis, Tennessee, in January 1968.

It soon became clear that one of the major issues facing the American government in Jordan was the continuing dispute between the Arabs and the people of Israel. As I went about the rounds to make initial contact with media and cultural officials, that problem was eventually brought up by all Jordanian officials that I met. They seemed eager to educate me and any other American official they came in contact with about their side of this continuing conflict.

When I visited professors at the University of Jordan, they too were always anxious to explain the great loss they had suffered due to their expulsion from their lands on the West Bank of the Jordan River, and they were just as emotional when discussing other lands that had been taken over by Israel. Under these circumstances, I could do only two things: first, survey the resources available at the American Cultural Center, and second, remind all of my contacts about the availability of the resources. I used the resources effectively to present the American government's positions on area problems that were of interest to educational and media leaders. Private individuals were also encouraged to use our facilities.

I made it a practice to take important political statements made by the secretary of state or leaders at the White House about the Middle East directly to editors of the local newspapers and to electronic media leaders. Often, when I went to hand-carry these kinds of documents to my media contacts, I would be asked to sit down for a while and talk about the Arab-Israeli problem. I always made it a practice to keep uppermost in my conversations the fact that I was there as a representative of the American government and had a duty to present and defend as effectively as possible the American government's position on all aspects of the Arab-Israeli dispute.

Governor William Scranton arrived in 1968 to try to advance peace talks between the Arabs and the Israelis. The picture below shows Governor Scranton and me as we headed for a press conference which I arranged for him at the American Cultural Center.

Dr. David Stratmon with governor of Pennsylvania William Scranton in Amman, Jordan, in December 1968

Although my Jordanian contacts in education and the media were usually opposed to the US government policy of supporting Israel within secure borders, they seemed resigned. This had been US policy over many decades, and there was no possibility that this American government policy would change even when the political leadership in the Congress and the White House changed from time to time. Moreover, a good many of the Jordanian leaders I talked with on a regular basis either had completed part of their education in America, had visited America, or had relatives who had visited or lived there over extended time periods. Their experiences in America and that of close relatives and friends reinforced my statements to them that a majority of the American people supported the US government's unswerving aid to and unchanging support of our ally, Israel.

I came to feel that our English-teaching program at the American Cultural Center was one of the most effective things we had going for us. Many Jordanians who had studied English in local schools came to the American Cultural Center to enroll in spoken-English classes. Perhaps Palestinians and Jordanians enrolled in our English classes to gain competency in English in the hope of landing a better job since they could add "fluency in English" to their resumes.

Our press section was usually able to get short features about various aspects of life in America placed on Jordanian television. The Fulbright Educational Exchange Program helped us explain America to many Jordanians. We sent many young as well as senior leaders from Jordan to America to make short orientation visits during which they would have the chance to get to know Americans who were doing the same kind of professional work as these carefully chosen Jordanians. The Fulbright Program also enabled us to bring to Jordan American speakers who were well-known personalities in their professional fields. We sent these American leaders to various parts of Jordan where they held formal and informal meetings with their professional colleagues, as well as with high school and college level students.

Burning of the American Cultural Center

In 1970, Assistant Secretary of State for Middle Eastern Affairs Mr. Joe Sisco was slated to come to the Republic of Jordan to discuss matters of mutual concern with King Hussein and other Jordanian leaders. Palestinian followers of Yasser Arafat began to stir up trouble in the streets in order to try to abort the scheduled visit. After many noisy demonstrations by El Fatah and other Palestinian groups, the visit by Mr. Sisco was still on track. The Palestinian leadership then resident in Jordan decided to send a stronger message to the American government. With that purpose in mind, a Palestinian mob took to the streets and marched to the American embassy. They shouted anti-American slogans, as well as anti-Israeli and anti-Joe Sisco slogans, as they marched. When the mob arrived at the American embassy compound, they set ablaze each of the vehicles in the parking lot at the embassy. When I heard that a mob had gathered at the American Cultural Center as I attended a meeting across town at the embassy, I got in my car and rushed back to the American Cultural Center.

When I arrived, I found that a screaming mob had indeed surrounded the bank building in which the cultural center was housed. Like the mob at the embassy, they were yelling and screaming anti-American slogans. They had taken over the street in front of the center, sent the Jordanian police packing, and had already prepared our cultural center for total destruction. When I arrived at the scene, I decided to approach the leader of the shouting mob and request his permission to enter the American Cultural Center to see if any member of my staff had been trapped inside the building. He agreed to let me go into the center for that purpose, and he made a way for me through the well-armed and angry mob.

I entered the building alone and searched every nook and cranny to see if some frightened employee was too cowered to make his or her escape through the unruly mob encircling the building. It was apparent to me, as I did a rapid walk through the building, that somebody had already poured some kind of incendiary agent over all of the books in the library and over all of the films in the film section and, in fact, had gone to great pains to make certain that when the blaze was lit, the fire would not stop until the entire center was destroyed. I am shown with some of the damage to our cultural center in the picture that follows.

Dr. David Stratmon, director of the American Cultural Center, looks over his office after an angry mob burned the center to protest a planned visit by Assistant Secretary of State Joe Sisco in February 1970

When I was satisfied that all of our American, Jordanian, and Palestinian employees were out of the building, I exited the front door through which I had entered. I thanked the leader of the mob for allowing me to make certain that nobody was trapped inside. I went across the street to call the embassy to make an initial report. A reporter from the *Chicago Tribune*, Michael McGuire, was there as well; and we engaged in a brief conversation. His account appeared in the April 16, 1970, issue on page 2. Michael described the burning of three American government-owned cars and a station wagon which were set afire within the embassy compound. However, he did not include my name in his account, but that is all right because I did not include his name in my report to government officials.

I watched as the building was destroyed by exploding dynamite and semiautomatic rifle fire. Apparently, the Jordanian government decided not to get involved in a fight with the Palestinians over the burning. The mob shouted with glee as the fire completely consumed what had been a beehive of activity. No fire truck came to fight the blaze, nor did any Jordanian police intercede to stop the destruction. When it was all over, the mob drifted away.

Much to my surprise on the next day, a Palestinian soldier, dressed in a fedayeen army field uniform, came marching up the hill to my house, which was located at the end of a dead-end street approximately two miles from the now-burned American Cultural Center. The young man was carrying a semiautomatic rifle in his right hand and had a hand grenade hanging from his army belt. I stepped outside my front door to greet him. He spoke in English, perhaps learned in the American Cultural Center English classes, and told me that what had happened to the American Cultural Center the previous day was "nothing personal" against me. However, if we opened up again, El Fatah would come and destroy the facility again. Then he bade me farewell, turned, and walked back down the hill to his vehicle.

With the help of the embassy administrative section, we soon found a new location for the cultural center, and we soon opened up again. Slowly, university students and others began to return for books or to reenroll in English classes. Our Fulbright Educational Exchange Program was soon actively engaged in promoting cultural exchange between America and Jordan, and eventually, we were up and running full steam. We did not have any more trouble from El Fatah or the rest of the Palestinian Liberation Organization (PLO).

Sadly, a young army officer who was the assistant military attaché was gunned down at his home in front of his pregnant wife and small son. That bloody incident in 1969 sent fear into the American families, especially those with small children who attended the American school. There was no protection against this kind of violence if it were directed at the American school. Fortunately, no additional acts of that sort happened during the remainder of the time my family and I lived in Jordan.

Chapter 13

Paris, France

After I graduated from the Department of Defense's National War College in Washington in 1971, I was appointed to serve at the American embassy in Paris until 1973.

Deputy Public Affairs Officer

Before I received clearance to go to Paris to assume my new position as deputy public affairs officer for the USIA cultural exchange program, I was ordered to fly to Paris to spend a weekend with the country public affairs officer, Burnett Anderson. The implication I drew from this kind of freedom with the taxpayers' money was that Burnett Anderson was a powerful man in the USIA, and if he wanted to look me over before starting the new assignment, that was the way it was going to be.

Although I did not like having to go that distance to be inspected, I kept my thoughts to myself and flew off to Paris because it was a requirement for the job. Burnett Anderson and his wife, Pia, could not have been more gracious. They insisted that I live in their apartment and take meals with their family. The two- or three-day ordeal was over soon enough, and I quickly settled into a Boeing 747 jet and headed back to Washington.

The job as deputy director of the large Information and Cultural Affairs Section of the American embassy in Paris was very interesting and demanding. While I was there, the final arrangements were being made to get America out of Vietnam with honor. The truce agreement that was put in place at the end of that costly war is still in place as I write. As the public affairs arm of the embassy in Paris, we had to provide the media, both written and electronic, with copies of all official statements by the American president and the secretary of state as quickly as we could produce French copies of the statements.

In addition, we closely monitored what the French newspapers, radio, and television programs were saying about political and economic issues that were important to top American officials. So we regularly filed summaries of what French media sources were broadcasting to people living in France and to the French-speaking world. By carefully reporting to Washington the results of this monitoring process, we helped the people who were backing up our information efforts in France, in French-speaking Africa, and other areas to "target" their output more effectively. It was important for the editorial writers in the Voice of America and in the press section of the USIA to know what statements by which officials had been slanted or truncated to such an extent that a listener in France or in French-speaking Africa or elsewhere in French-speaking communities around the world might draw a conclusion that was vastly different from what the American government was saying and doing about a world problem. To keep up with this job, we had to work very hard, but it was enjoyable work.

We also had to work closely with the joint American-French Fulbright Committee that gave policy guidance and direction to the large educational exchange program that was being operated in the early 1970s.

Chief Justice Warren Burger

Director of Public Affairs Burnett Anderson was an old friend of Chief Justice Warren Burger. Anderson had been handpicked by Justice Burger to edit his papers. Anderson was to start as soon as he retired from the USIA. On occasions when Justice Burger would arrive in Paris for a short visit, Anderson would sometimes ask me to meet him at the airport in our chauffeur-driven limousine and ride with him to Anderson's home where he stayed on two occasions. On one occasion, I had the honor of arranging for the chief justice to come to our office and speak to our American and French staff. He very graciously agreed to come and discuss the US Supreme Court and the appellate court system. Afterward, he stayed long enough to answer questions.

Louis "Satchmo" Armstrong

When the great trumpeter Louis "Satchmo" Armstrong died in 1971, a delegation of French jazz musicians came to the American embassy and requested permission to celebrate his passing by giving a concert in his honor at the American embassy. The public affairs section of the embassy was delighted to get this kind of positive publicity because it would help counteract some of the bad taste that lingered in Europe and in France over the role the Americans played in the Vietnam War.

Ambassador John Watson listened to arguments on both sides of this impromptu jazz matter. Public Affairs thought it was something we should seize upon and exploit to the fullest, but security officials in the embassy were able to carry the day. Ambassador Watson decided to deny permission for the jazz concert to take place inside or near the US embassy grounds. The ambassador's father was the founder of IBM, and he received his appointment as US ambassador to Paris after he made a generous contribution to President Nixon's political campaign. When the musicians were not allowed to play at the embassy, they announced that they would go to the Luxembourg Gardens and pay a musical homage there. I followed the jazzmen to the Luxembourg Gardens. A crowd gathered at that beautiful park where the jazzmen took out their musical instruments which included two trumpets, a clarinet, and a trombone. They assumed a reverent stance and began to play. The sounds seemed to float across the afternoon breeze as they played one verse of "The Muskrat's Ramble." Then they carefully returned their instruments to their carrying cases and, to the utter dismay of the small crowd, slipped away.

The crowd tried, but they could not get the jazz ensemble to play any additional music. Just one verse wafted on the still Parisian air to mark the passing of one of the world's greatest jazz musicians. Afterward, the musicians disappeared into the afternoon crowd. Louis would have been pleased with that beautifully staged tribute.

Chapter 14

Tunis, Tunisia

Tunis is a plethora of ancient palaces which include mosques and centers of trade and learning. The Tunisian economy has grown much in recent years, and living standards are among Africa's highest. President Zine El Abidine Ben Ali, elected in November 1987, initiated several major reforms anchoring democracy and enlarging political participation. My role was dual as director of the American Cultural Center and as counselor of Embassy for Public Affairs from 1973 to 1975.

Director and Counselor

Under the leadership of President Habib Bourguiba in the '70s, Tunisia was a country that had no axe to grind with the US government or with Americans in general. The early '70s were a good time to serve as director of the American Cultural Center. We were still in the Cold War era, and everybody at American embassies around the world had to be alert to make sure that Washington was not blindsided by some act by Russian diplomats that was hostile to American worldwide interests.

President Habib Bourguiba, first president of modern Tunisia, and Dr. David L. Stratmon Sr., counselor of Embassy for Public Affairs and director of the American Cultural Center, Tunis, Tunisia, 1975

The officials in the ministries of education and information were always glad to see me or members of my American Cultural Center staff when we contacted them to provide and discuss texts of statements by American government officials and leaders from elsewhere in American society. Editors of newspapers and electronic media seemed especially glad to have official texts of statements by the American president, secretary of state, and the US defense department. They apparently liked to check statements provided by Eastern bloc nations' diplomats against what had really been said by American leaders concerning political and economic issues that were of possible interest to their Tunisian audiences. So each day, we translated into Arabic almost all of the important statements that were sent overnight to our cultural center press section from Washington via our wireless file. By cultivating good relations with media and educational leaders, we were able to hand-carry official texts of statements from leaders in Washington that were most timely and early enough for the deadlines that Tunisian media outlets had to meet.

James Keogh (left), director of USIA, Washington, DC; Dr. David Stratmon (right), counselor of Embassy for Public Affairs, American embassy, Tunis, Tunisia; Bill Pugh (center), deputy assistant director, USIA for the Middle East and North Africa. This photo was taken during the Public Affairs Officers Conference at Tunis, Tunisia, in October 1974

Our American Cultural Center library had thousands of volumes in English, French, and Arabic which were available for Tunisian teachers, students, and others who wanted to broaden their grasp and understanding of American life, whether it is political, educational, economic, social, or historical. We tried to make our books and films readily available; and we sought to make sure that the center library and other facilities were clean, attractively decorated, and altogether the kind of quiet environment where young and old alike, including men and women, would feel comfortable while reading periodical literature or studying all aspects of life in America.

Ambassador Talcott Williams Seelye (left), an unidentified official, Foreign Minister Chatti of Tunisia, and Dr. David Stratmon present moon rocks to Tunisian president Habib Bourguiba

American ambassador Talcott Williams Seelye asked me to accompany him to several meetings with President Bourguiba. Those meetings were usually held at the presidential palace. Once we presented the president with a gift of moon rocks which were collected from the moon and returned to earth aboard an American spacecraft. Activities such as this helped to seal the friendship of the American and the Tunisians.

Russian Diplomats

The American Cultural Center in Tunis drew the attention of Russian diplomats. They noticed that we could fill our language classes and library. I guess they wondered how we could keep a constant stream of readers visiting the library to spend time reading about American history, literature, government, and capitalism while their library seemed almost deserted.

One day, when I was attending a cocktail party at the West German embassy, an operative from the Russian embassy struck up a conversation with me and eventually said he would like to come over for a tour of the American Cultural Center to see how we did it. He wanted to know how we were able to attract so many Tunisians to our cultural center on a daily basis. I immediately told the American ambassador about the interest of the Russian embassy operative in visiting the American Cultural Center. The ambassador and I agreed on a time when we would invite him. I called and assured the Russian that he would be welcome. On the appointed day, the Russian diplomat arrived, and I began to give him a tour of our multilingual library. About halfway through the tour, a young Arab male stood up and took a flash photograph of me and the diplomat. He was so startled that he left the building running! Russian embassy officials in Tunisia kept away after that.

Foreign Service Career Ends

When my family and I left Tunisia in the summer of 1975 and flew to Southampton, England, where we took Queen Elizabeth II home to America, we marked the end of a long and interesting period of service abroad as a US Foreign Service information officer. After a few weeks of home leave, I served for a while as a senior foreign policy specialist in the Africa division of the US State Department. This was an unexciting and lackluster position, and I immediately started to look around for ways to get out of it.

I transferred to the Cultural Affairs-Africa Office of the US State Department and served for over a year as deputy director of the Fulbright Program south of the Sahara. I relished that assignment in part because it gave me an opportunity to serve once again with US Foreign Service officer James Relph. He had been deputy chief of the mission in Tunisia when I served there as director of the American Cultural Center in the early 1960s. I also enjoyed using our allocation of Fulbright Program dollars to encourage American cultural and educational institutions to establish links with their African counterparts.

Later, I was asked to serve on a selection panel with the State Department Officer Selection Board. I appreciated that assignment because it gave me the opportunity to have a direct input into the selection of the next batch of US Foreign Service officers for both the State Department and the USIA. The year I served as part of the selection process, 2,300 candidates had passed the foreign service officer written examination which is administered in December of each year in cities in various parts of the country. After extensive training, those of us who served as members of the interview panels traveled across the country and interviewed applicants who had passed the written examination.

We used an All-Day Assessment Center process to find the top 10 percent of candidates. In effect, our job was to select the best 230 officers we could find from the 2,300 who were successful on the written examination. Each time we interviewed ten young candidates, we knew that, in effect, only one of that group could pass. We made our recommendations based on our intensive all-day written and oral exam process. The final selection was made by the personnel divisions of the US State Department and the USIA in Washington, DC.

I was deeply impressed with the caliber of the candidates who came before us hoping for acceptance into the US Foreign Service Officer Corps.US Foreign Service Officer Corps *See* US Foreign Service Information Officer Such high-quality candidates meant that the future of our country was going to be in good hands. If this country can continue to produce the well-educated and highly motivated cadre of young Americans who are willing to serve wherever they are sent to protect US interests abroad, then it certainly appears that our international affairs will be well administered.

Chapter 15

Post-Foreign Service Activities

After I retired from the US Foreign Service, I embarked on several new adventures. Some of my new activities included the following: coordinator of the Cooperative Education Program at the Smithsonian Institution, chair of the Washington, DC citywide fund-raising campaign for the American Red Cross, a real estate salesman for DEAR Realty, and a professor of political science at Rust College. After my wife of fifty years died, I remarried a lovely lady, Lillian Jean, who has spiced up my senior years.

Coordinator of Smithsonian Cooperative Education Program

Just before I retired from the US Foreign Service, I was delighted to learn that the Office of Personnel at the Smithsonian Institution was searching for someone to head up its new Cooperative Education Program. I went to the Smithsonian and filled out a lengthy application for that job and eventually was asked to meet a selection panel. Based on that panel's recommendation, I signed a two-year contract. My employment commenced directly after I left the USIA.

My last day with the USIA was on a Friday in July 1979, and I reported to Mr. Will Douglas's office the following Monday. Mr. Douglas was director of the Office of Minority Affairs, and the Cooperative Education Program was to be operated under the direct control of the Office of Minority Affairs. I was pleased with the office space that came with my new job. From my office window in the Smithsonian's Old Castle Building on the mall in Washington, I could look out onto the buildings which housed the Congress, and it was only a short walk from the Smithsonian to the White House.

Historically, the Smithsonian had not hired many African Americans, nor many other nonwhite minorities and only a relatively few women for senior service. Women had been systemically denied promotion to such positions as museum directors by a rigid ceiling that was very much a fact of life at that time. I visited and held discussions with the heads of these components: the director of the National Zoo, the director of the National Portrait Gallery, and with Smithsonian officials on the Harvard University campus who collaborate with the national space scientists at Harvard, and the director of each of the Smithsonian major museums located on the Washington mall.

Some of these top people at the Smithsonian said without reservation that they had never known an African American who had the kind of skills they needed at the Smithsonian. I discussed the possibility of hiring a nonwhite intern under the new Cooperative Education Program with several unconvinced people. For example, the deputy director of the National Zoo, which is part of the

Smithsonian and located in the nation's capital city, was absolutely opposed to the whole idea. When I mentioned the fine veterinary medicine program at Tuskegee Institute in Alabama, and queried him about the possibility of an intern coming to the Zoo, he made short of the idea by saying that as far as he knew, African American youth never had the experience of growing up with a close relative who was a "bird-watcher." This meant, he said, that there was no pool of candidates growing up in the African American communities across America who would later possess the kind of skills and love of animals that develop when you have been taught to love and respect animals by accompanying a close relative on bird-watching expeditions. It is hard to deal with that kind of deep-seated ethnic prejudice.

Fortunately, I was able to find several museum directors and other senior officials who were willing to have interns provided they were allowed to have a voice in making the final selection. With that small opening in what seemed to be an impregnable wall against minorities, we prepared notices about our new Smithsonian Internship Program and went out to beat the bushes at colleges and universities for likely candidates. As responses came in, I arranged to visit college campuses to discuss the program with college officials and students. Among the campuses I visited were Harvard, Michigan State, UCLA, the University of North Carolina, Hampton Institute, Jackson State University, Rust College, North Carolina A&T State University, and Howard University. A committee at the Smithsonian carried out an initial review of the applications and chose those who appeared to have the greatest potential. Eventually, we were able to offer temporary employment as interns to only two of the many candidates. A white female from the University of North Carolina came to the budget office, and an African American female science major from Jackson State University located in Jackson, Mississippi, was placed in the Museum of Natural History.

The Smithsonian is only partly under the control of the federal government. When that institution was set up, it was chartered as an institution that was partly private with its own board of trustees, private funding from money left to it by Smithson, the Englishman who had left his fortune to set up an institution for the diffusion of knowledge in America. The Smithsonian uses funds left by Mr. Smithson and federal government money. Since about half of its funding comes from private sources, it has never been completely under the control of the federal government.

Historically, whenever the Smithsonian has not wanted to abide by any federal regulation or mandate that it found unacceptable, the chair of the board of trustees has simply written to whatever federal agency was trying to push them in a direction it chose not to go. By written communication, they were reminded that the Smithsonian is a "private agency" and is not required to follow all federal rules that were applicable to regular federal agencies. That tactic has usually been enough to keep the federal government from completely imposing its personnel system on the Smithsonian. However, in the late 1970s, many officials at the Smithsonian also alluded to the government-wide freeze on hiring then in effect that restricted their ability to consider new hires that might be brought aboard through the new Cooperative Education Program.

By the time my two-year contract expired in 1981, it was clear to me that the Smithsonian was not yet ready to move forward with an internship program that could bring minorities aboard faster than the entrenched Smithsonian bureaucracy was ready to receive them. There was no office in the federal government at that time with the clout or inclination to nudge the Smithsonian away from that "go slow" position where minorities were concerned.

Despite our best efforts, it was just not possible in the late 1970s and early 1980s to get an effective Coop Education Program off and running at the Smithsonian. The government-wide hiring freeze that the Office of Personnel Management had imposed throughout the federal government at about that time did not make our job any easier. I hope that our efforts will be viewed by history as groundwork for the future.

Chair of the American Red Cross Campaign

In 1984, some friends with whom I had worked on the Howard University Institutional Review Board asked me to accept the unpaid position of chair of the citywide fund-raising campaign for the American Red Cross. I accepted the job and arranged to meet with people who had been involved in the fund-raiser during the previous year. We developed a plan in which the city of Washington would be divided into four quadrants, and former volunteers would work in the four quadrants. Since we did not have funds with which to purchase publicity, we made skillful use of the free written and electronic media. We also worked out a plan to solicit help from community organizations such as churches, schools, and other community-based local groups. We planned to raise the bulk of our contributions from door-to-door campaigning.

Organizing each city block, ward, and precinct with chairmen/ chairwomen was an arduous task. Once our teams began to knock on doors throughout Washington, we held weekly meetings with groups of our foot soldiers. It became apparent early on that many of our volunteers were discouraged by the lack of generosity they were encountering when they telephoned and/or knocked on doors to ask for donations. We realized, too late, that we should have hired a professional fund-raiser and used more professional fund-raising techniques. When we finished counting the money, we found that we had raised a little over $5,000 from the nation's 1984 capital city fund-raiser. Clearly, a lot of our volunteer fund-raisers simply gave up the chase after a few doors were closed in their faces and after experiencing too many unpleasant telephone responses. This campaign turned out to be a training program for me as well as for all the volunteers who worked so hard.

Salesman for DEAR Realty

Around 1980, Freddie Mae heard about night classes in real estate that the DEAR Realty Company in Washington was conducting. She suggested that I check out this possibility for employment. I enrolled, and at the end of a six-week course, I passed the real estate salesman exam, and I began to work for DEAR Realty at its Upper Northwest office which was located only a few blocks from our home. At that time, we lived in a ten-room house on Alaska Avenue. I found the real estate business to be very dull. I spent almost every Sunday showing properties all over Northwest Washington to so-called prospective buyers, almost none of whom had any real intention of buying a house. It soon dawned on me that many folks considered looking at houses for sale as a Sunday afternoon outing. When I became adept at picking clients by first "prequalifying" them, or at least checking to see if they had the necessary financial resources, I stopped wasting my time and gas taking would-be customers to see houses that they had no intention of purchasing.

Later, I took real estate courses in the evening at the University of Maryland, and that prepared me to pass the Maryland brokers' examination. With that additional qualification to hang on the walls of DEAR Realty's main office, I began to show properties to prospective customers in Maryland as well as Washington, but with only marginal success. Before long, I got the message that I was never going to become a hotshot real estate salesman.

I took consolation in the fact that I had purchased and almost completed paying for several houses in my hometown of Southport and in Washington while I was still in the USIA. Those properties became a large part of my retirement package in later years. If I had realized in the 1960s how these properties would appreciate when "white flight" was occurring from Washington to the suburbs of Virginia and Maryland, I could have salted away a dozen single family houses for very little cash up front to help assure my retirement security. As it was, I did purchase three such houses in Northwest Washington while I was still in the US Foreign Service, and all three of these properties increased at least ten times over their original cost. For me, the real estate that I purchased over forty years ago paid off much more handsomely in terms of appreciation in value than did any of the investments I made over the years in the stock market.

The real secret to my financial good fortune has to be the fact that my first wife, Freddie Mae, was an excellent money manager. She always knew which tenant was not paying on time, when it was prudent to invest in yet another rental property, and when it was time to double up on monthly mortgage payments to increase our equity in our real estate holdings. I never made a move in real estate or the stock market for that matter if she was not in favor of the purchase or sale that was in question.

The one exception to that rule was my decision to invest heavily in a subdivision of home building sites in Holly Springs, Mississippi. My partner and I did not do sufficient preliminary study to forecast the market for middle-class homes before we invested a large chunk of our retirement savings in a thirty-one-lot subdivision. Lots in that subdivision sold slowly. However, we were able to sell ten lots at one time through a grant awarded to the Holly Springs Housing Authority. We took solace in the fact that we paid for the land outright and, therefore, did not have to make mortgage payments. I will revisit this topic later.

Professor and Chair

While I was trying to get my career as a real estate salesman and broker off to a good start, I ran into my old friend Dr. W. A. McMillan, president of Rust College. Rust was founded in 1866 by the Freedman's Aid Society of the United Methodist Church, and it is a United Methodist Church-related educational institution. Dr. McMillan was attending a conference in Washington, and he advised me that Rust could use the services of someone with my academic credentials and experience. He asked if I was interested in coming to Rust College. My wife was only lukewarm to the idea of packing up and moving again after so many moves while we were with the USIA. Also she was enjoying her job with the USIA Office of the General Counsel. Be that as it may, we finally decided to accept Dr. McMillan's employment offer.

When we arrived in Holly Springs, Mississippi, in the fall of 1984, Dr. McMillan had arranged housing for us on Randolph Street directly bordering the east side of the Rust College campus. He also arranged for Freddie Mae to work in the registrar's office. As soon as we unpacked our household effects from the U-Haul trailer that we towed from Washington behind our Dodge Dart sedan, and enrolled our youngest child in CADET Catholic School, we were ready to go to work. Our other children were all grown and living independently.

I was glad to get back into classroom teaching again. I had taught political science for a year at Prairie View A&M College (now University) just before I went abroad with the USIA in 1956. My job at Rust College gave me an opportunity to draw upon the wealth of experience I had gained in my foreign service career. Students enjoyed hearing about the political conditions in Ghana, Chad, Morocco, Tunisia, Congo, Lebanon, Jordan, and France.

In addition, I had spent two years studying Arabic at the Foreign Service Institute in Beirut, Lebanon; and I had spent another year studying US national security issues while enrolled at the National War College. I was in the class of 1971. I also enrolled in several classes at the American University of Beirut while I was stationed in Lebanon between 1959 and 1961. While there, I gained a good grasp of the historical roots of Islam including a study of the life of Muhammad, and I had an opportunity to read through the Holy Koran with the help of scholars at the University of Beirut. I learned to appreciate the role of oil in the economies and lives of the people of the Middle East as well.

I was able to introduce a seminar on Middle Eastern affairs to the curriculum at Rust, which I taught to upperclassmen. It required students to keep current with whatever was headline news about the Middle East by listening to selected newscasts, especially National Public Radio and the major networks' news analysis programs. They had to read texts and periodical literature that informed them about the ancient land of the Fertile Crescent.

I enjoyed the constitutional law seminars that I offered for junior and senior social science majors which included a few prelaw and political science majors. During the first week of these seminars, I supplied students with a list of fifty constitutional law cases. We analyzed and dissected these cases throughout the semester.

The Rust administrators asked me teach a business law course, and I was pleased to do that. I always announced on the first day of class that we would cover every case and every page of our large textbook during the eight-week module. So everybody had to dig in and begin serious study from the beginning. I would then go through the first several chapters and assign cases to individual students. When we reached those cases, the assigned students were expected to be our in-house experts for the assigned cases. Students were expected to be ready to answer any questions asked by me or the class about the business law issues raised by the case or cases that had been assigned.

Whenever I could find a banker, insurance professional, attorney, or any other person living in the area with experience and knowledge about business law, I would ask them to come and spend an hour with my students. My brother-in-law and trucking company owner, Jesse Wilson, conducted several of these sessions. The question-and-answer session was especially appealing to the students, one of whom entered the trucking industry after he graduated. He now owns and drives an eighteen-wheeler. Jesse has had more than forty-five years' experience in owning and operating eighteen-wheel trucks. Jesse proved to be an excellent storyteller, and the students loved him.

I also had the opportunity to teach such basic political science courses as American government, state and local government, comparative government, political parties, and political theory. I took pleasure in teaching each of these courses and always tried to find local politicians or other resource persons to share their experiences with my students.

Each Rust College student was required to take a course called Social Science Seminar during the freshman or sophomore year. That seminar was designed to give each student an appreciation of the major social science issues such as the following: where humans came from and how they moved from a state of nature to civilized local and national groups. Other topics were how various societies handle issues about the family, religion, and education; the origins of race and culture; forms of government; how various social groups make a living; and how nations, states, and other political entities interact with each other in the international arena.

During the time I was head of the Social Science Division, I had the good fortune to invite several outstanding retired educators to help us train students. A half dozen or so such dedicated educators came to Rust. Among them were Dr. Molly Schuchett, anthropologist, who lived in retirement in Washington, DC; Dr. Albert Gray from Berea, Ohio; and Mr. Mahlon T. Puryear, from Hampton, Virginia.

Unlike Drs. Schuchett and Gray, Mr. Puryear came to Rust for one week each year, beginning in 1989 and continuing through the 2004 academic year. Drs. Schuchett and Gray each spent two academic years as volunteer professors working in the Social Science Division while I was the chair. None of them charged Rust College anything for their unselfish service to our students; and each, in his or her own way, made a huge contribution to broadening the horizons of our students by bringing their wealth of experience as college professors or as a senior official of the National Urban League as was the case with Mr. Puryear. Mr. Puryear added depth to our curriculum based on his experience as a senior official of the National Urban League. Dr. and Mrs. Gray even established a scholarship fund to help graduates in the social sciences continue their education beyond Rust College.

We had limited financial resources for student travel, but we were able to have one young male student spend a summer in a village in rural Kenya, thanks to the Operations Crossroads Africa program which Rev. and Mrs. James Robinson of New York started several decades ago. We also found the wherewithal for one of our political science majors to spend a year studying at Oxford University in England. Afterward, he returned to complete his BA degree at Rust College before entering Harvard for study leading to the masters and PhD in political science.

Each year, we were always able to use the Rust College bus to take forty or more students to visit the Parchman Farm penitentiary system at Parchman, Mississippi. It was always a powerful learning experience for our young people to visit Parchman Farm where they listened to briefings by inmates about what life is like inside that kind of institution for people who stray away from acceptable behavior. Further, they revealed how their use of illegal drugs eventually led to their incarceration.

Years later, former chief justice Warren Burger was appointed to head the US Bicentennial Commission and help prepare the bicentennial celebration of 1989 to honor the adoption of the US Constitution in 1789. When the Bicentennial Commission sent out a request that programs be planned nationwide to help celebrate the adoption of the Constitution, I wrote a proposal requesting funds from the US Bicentennial Commission to defray costs of a two-day workshop that would diffuse information about the US Constitution to high school teachers in Marshall County where I was then employed as a professor of political science at Rust College.

The Bicentennial Commission approved our request, and we put our program into effect. One of the highlights of that workshop was the presentation of a pamphlet-size copy of the US Constitution to each participating high school teacher and principal. I had written to former chief justice Burger and reminded him of our contacts in Paris over fifteen years earlier through the offices of our mutual friend Burnett Anderson. I requested, and he personally signed thirty copies of the Constitution for presentation to each of the thirty workshop participants.

It was exciting for each of the workshop participants, all of whom were teachers and principals in the Marshall County School System, to receive a copy of the US Constitution autographed by a former chief justice of the United States Supreme Court. Mr. Burger served on the US Supreme Court during the period 1969-1986. It was my hope that these copies of the US Constitution would become family heirlooms for each of the participating educators.

During the eleven years I was privileged to be a part of the faculty at this outstanding school, I received more than I was able to give back. Beyond a doubt, the work we did at Rust was more satisfying to me and to my deceased wife, Freddie Mae, than any employment we ever had prior to our arrival in the summer of 1984. I continue to thank God for giving us this chance to finish our professional careers by helping train young minds.

I have been active in politics. Unsuccessfully, I ran for the office of Alderman representing the second ward, and I served on the board of the Marshall County Democratic Executive Committee for eight years. I helped Mayor Eddie Lee Smith to get elected by recruiting students to staff phone banks, supply transportation to the polls, and canvass neighborhoods by campaigning door to door. The former mayor and the new mayor are shown the picture below.

Outgoing mayor John Dabney Brown congratulates incoming mayor Eddie Lee Smith on July 3, 1989, as Dr. David Stratmon looks on. Mayor Smith was the first black mayor of Holly Springs, Mississippi

DW Estates Subdivision

Dr. W. A. McMillan, president emeritus of Rust College, and I decided early in the 1990s that we would either build an apartment complex or a subdivision on homesites in Holly Springs. Eventually, we purchased a thirty-one-acre site within the city limits, took bids from prospective builders for the subdivision, and eventually hired Carl Parker, a builder from North Carolina, who submitted the lowest bid. Carl is a Rust College graduate and is a nephew of Dr. McMillan.

After the subdivision was completed early in 1992, we discovered that we had not done enough research prior to sinking over $360,000 of our retirement money into this venture. Although we advertised widely in the local area, including Shelby and Marshall County, we still had difficulty selling the lots. Many people used our time showing the lots and working on deals that later fell through. A huge problem was getting people to qualify for a loan through a bank or mortgage company; and we were, therefore, left with twenty-three unsold lots on which we had to pay taxes of around $4,000 each year. Fortunately, we did not owe a mortgage or any other building costs. We paid as we went, but we still had to dig into our pockets each year at tax-paying time.

The lesson of our subdivision experience is that educators ought to investigate carefully before investing their retirement money in subdivisions in low-income towns like Holly Springs. If the demand for affordable housing and building sites is not large enough, the houses and lots you build in a subdivision may remain unsold for a long time.

Spice for my Senior Years

After Freddie Mae's death in 1998, I was very lonely. I spent my days eating peanut butter sandwiches and watching television. I logged on to the computer dating Web sites and described what I would like in a companion. A lady responded, and after a short conversation, we arranged a place and time for a date. Unfortunately, she got cold feet and called the date off, so I will never know what that dear lady looked like. Next, I surveyed the church since I really wanted someone who shared my Catholic religious beliefs.

I noticed a lady who collected the offerings at Saturday mass, so I attended Saturday mass more frequently even though I never missed singing in the Sunday choir. During the Mass, I would make my way over to her side of the sanctuary in order to look her over a little better. One Saturday, I decided to sit next to her, and enjoying this, I eventually proposed, and we were married on October 19, 1999. Of course, the story is a little longer than that, but you don't need to know everything.

Dr. David Stratmon and Dr. Lillian Jean Stratmon

Lillian Jean's interests are similar to mine in many ways. Besides being Catholic converts, we have received doctorate degrees and share hobbies such as music and gardening. She also likes to sew and cook. I enjoy having my clothes repaired, and I like to eat. At the age of sixteen, she was awarded a $20,000 scholarship upon her graduation from St. Mary's Catholic High School in Holly Springs, Mississippi. She graduated from Alverno College in Milwaukee, Wisconsin, in 1959 with a degree in business education. Her master's degree is from Louisiana State University at New Orleans, and her doctorate was awarded by the University of Southern Mississippi. Just as I was department chair at Rust College, Lillian Jean was department chair and faculty senate president at Southern University at New Orleans. She rose to the rank of full professor. After completing twenty-eight years there, she retired and became a professor of education and business at Rust College in Holly Springs.

After we were married, we spent three weeks traveling through Israel, Jordan, Syria, and other countries of the Middle East during our honeymoon. Our tour leader, a Catholic priest, prepared a prayerful and spiritual adventure that fed the soul and the senses. We visited the place where Jesus was believed to be born, and we were baptized in the Jordan River. We carried the cross up Golgotha along the same streets traveled by Jesus as he struggled toward the hilltop where He was crucified. We collected olive and mustard seeds from the Mount of Olives outside Jerusalem. Bethany and Bethlehem were also on our agenda. The tour covered so many biblical places that the trip can be summed up as "a walk through the Bible."

Dr. David Stratmon and Dr. Lillian Jean Stratmon
at the Sea of Galilee

Returning home to Mississippi, we set up house on Swaney Road even though Lillian Jean owned a large house a few blocks away. She had enjoyed decorating, gardening, and playing piano when I met her; and she continued these activities when we moved in together. She began playing the piano for masses on Saturdays, and I sometimes led the congregation in singing. Many people noticed our mutual enjoyment of music and invited us to provide entertainment for weddings, funerals, and parties. We took part in the production of plays and Mardi Gras celebrations at St. Joseph Catholic Church.

A few years passed, and we were ready for another overseas trip. In 2001, we "followed in the footsteps of St. Paul" with the same group of Catholic travelers with whom we had traveled to the Middle East. This time, we journeyed throughout Greece and Turkey. Actually, it was a continuation of our biblical sojourn; and we toured such ancient sites as the following: Athens, Corinth, Veria, Thessaloniki, Macedonia, Istanbul, Alexandria, Sardis, Philadelphia, Ephesus, Patmos, Crete, and many other places. We traveled by van, bus, boat, cruise liner, and foot. Back in our home church of St. Joseph's, we showed our films and pictures to the congregation.

Dr. David Stratmon and Dr. Lillian Stratmon at the house
of Mary, the mother of Jesus, at Ephesus in Turkey

We have traveled around the United States to many functions and family gatherings. Since I am a member of the Omega Psi Phi and the Sigma Pi Phi fraternities, we have been active at local and national gatherings. Lillian Jean is a member of the Sigma Gamma Rho sorority, and she works with several organizations doing civic and community work. This busy life has kept us excited about each new day. Some places we would like to visit in the future are Brazil, Canada, and China.

PART III

Chapter 16

Musings of a Senior Citizen

Since this is my autobiography, I get to say what I want. So this is the part in which I just "muse" about a few things, but mostly it explains experiences which shaped me spiritually. "Religious Traveling," "Little White Sisters of Africa," "*Confessions* and *City of God*," and "Sixteenth Street Unitarian Church" are the headings that I use for the purpose of organization.

Religious Traveling

All the different places we traveled to and the different religious experiences we have had caused me to call this section "Religious Traveling." There is no other reason for this title.

When I grew up in Southport between the mid-1920s until I graduated from high school in 1941, all the black folks in town were members of one of three church groups: African Methodist Episcopal Zion, African Methodist Episcopal, or Baptist. Nobody in the black community seemed to be Episcopalian, Presbyterian, or Catholic. I had never even heard anybody discuss the Catholic Church, except Monsignor Fulton J. Sheen. Aunt Eva Lee and her husband, Charles W. Lee, used to listen to Monsignor Sheen almost every Sunday afternoon on their radio, but they were both pillars of the St. James AMEZ Church in Southport. Indeed, by tradition, all the members of my immediate family in Southport were expected to attend, or at least support financially, the St. James AMEZ Church.

My grandmother, Mame, considered herself a supporter of St. James too, but I never knew her to venture out of the yard during the entire fourteen years I spent with her. However, Mame saw to it that my brother and I attended both the 11:00 a.m. service and the 2:00 p.m. Sunday school at St. James every Sunday.

The question of which church I would attend was never an issue until 1948 when Freddie Mae and I spent two years working and living in Monrovia, Liberia. While there, the small cluster of Americans who worked for the US Public Health Service Mission arranged to worship along with our family at a Sunday service presided over by Chappie Faulkner. Chappie had been a chaplain in the US military during World War II and was a resident of Liberia.

In Lebanon, we became associated with an informal Bible study group that met at various homes on Sundays. Often we arranged to travel together to visit historical sites in or near Beirut as part of the service. These Sunday excursions gave us an opportunity to visit several of the crusader castles which still stand as forlorn monuments to efforts by Western powers to establish and maintain control over distant lands and peoples.

When my family and I were in Fort Lamy, Chad, from 1963 to 1965, we began to attend Sunday morning service at the local Catholic Church. Later between 1971 and 1973, when we were in Paris, we attended a Catholic church where the service was in English. Mainly Americans and other English-speaking foreigners attended this service. Some of the priests were Irish.

While in Tunis, Tunisia, from 1973 to 1975, we were regulars at a large Catholic church that was administered by the Dominican priests. The services were in French, but by then, we were completely at ease in a French-speaking environment, and we followed the Mass easily in French. Part of our routine in Tunis was to visit the home of retired foreign service officer Will Smith every Sunday morning and take him to Mass with us. Will had decided to live in Tunis in his retirement. He lived in a large wall-enclosed house with a well in the front yard that dated from Roman times. Will employed only one faithful servant, Ahmed, who had looked after Will for many years. Will had been blind and living in Tunis for several years when we met him in 1973. He had a colossal storehouse of knowledge about the history and politics of Tunisia and North Africa. Besides that, he was a good storyteller. He threw the best party in town at Christmas each year with hundreds of guests, including both Tunisians and non-Tunisian friends. When Will Smith died during our tour of duty in Tunis, I felt as though I had lost a close family member.

These experiences with religion in so many different settings have shaped my philosophy of life. It has given me the ability to view people in a detached way, yet with empathy, which allows me to understand and sympathize with just about everyone, including those who despise me.

Little White Sisters of Africa

When I was assigned to the US Public Health Service Mission in Monrovia, Freddie Mae and I visited the leprosy colony in up-country Liberia. The colony was located a short distance from the Firestone rubber tree plantation, and we traveled for about two hours over very poor roads before reaching the plantation. I had been told that "the Catholics run the leprosy colony." When we arrived at the financially strapped place, we found that the "little white sisters of Africa" were the managers and operators. They gave us a tour and explained their work. There was no cure for leprosy, so the sisters seemed dedicated to making their patients comfortable while they awaited their inevitable death. For some, the illness disfigured them, and it had eaten away some of the body parts of others.

Some of the Catholic nuns had not left the leprosy colony for home leave in over ten years, but they seemed cheerful and totally dedicated to their mission of helping to heal the sick. We came away with tremendous admiration for these dedicated sisters who knew that some of them would die of one kind of disease or another right there in the leprosy colony without ever seeing their loved ones at home again. That did not make them complain or be less energetic in carrying out what they obviously considered to be the will of God. I have never seen any other missionaries in any of the countries I visited while assigned to Africa who worked so cheerfully under such abominable conditions. Their example of selfless service to the downtrodden had a tremendous effect on my decision many years later to become a Catholic.

Confessions and *City of God*

Saint Augustine tells us in his *Confessions* about his early life in North Africa and Italy. His father was a provincial official of the Roman Empire and was stationed in the small city of Tegaste, which is located in what is now modern Algeria. As a young man, Augustine spread his wild oats. He provides readers with a great deal of information about that part of his life in his informative book that he called *Confessions*.

During that part of his life, he fathered a child out of wedlock, and although he never married the young lady, he did take care of his acknowledged son. Indeed, when Augustine founded a religious order, he brought his son into the fold and personally guided him into a religious life, which is something his own father had not done for him. In fact, he tells us that although his mother, Monica, was a very religious woman and kept after her son, Augustine, until he reformed his ways and became a good Catholic, she was not able to get Augustine's dad to amend his ways and become a follower of Christ until he was practically at death's door. After Augustine converted to Catholicism, he rose quickly to become a Catholic bishop with his headquarters located at the North African town of Hippo.

What first attracted me to this giant of a philosopher and thinker was a term paper I completed about early church leaders while I was enrolled in the graduate school at the University of Michigan in the early 1950s.

Dr. James Meisel, professor of political science in the Horace Rackham Graduate School at Michigan, suggested to his political theory students that "somebody ought to do a paper on the early church fathers." I had never heard of the early church fathers, but I went to the library directly after class and looked up "early church fathers." At that time, I was still a member of the African Methodist Episcopal Zion Church. I quickly became thoroughly immersed in my study of the early church fathers as I prepared my term paper on this subject. While studying the early church fathers, I picked up a copy of Augustine's *City of God* and completed reading it in a few days.

By the time I finished reading that book, I felt a kinship with St. Augustine which still continues today more than fifty years after I first read *City of God*. By AD 410, the Roman Empire had suffered defeat; and Rome, the capital city, was sacked by the Goths and other foes. Before long, critics were looking for someone to blame for the crushing defeat of the great and mighty Roman Empire, which had been around since the second century before the birth of Christ.

Eventually, many critics of the church began to say that the reason the empire had fallen was because it had turned its back on the gods of old who had stood by the Roman Empire as it rose to world domination. When the Roman emperor Constantine I in AD 313 decided to become a Christian himself, i.e., become a Catholic, Constantine required that the cross of Christ adorn the banners carried aloft by Roman soldiers as they engaged their enemies. That signaled to the gods of old, critics said, that Rome had turned its back on the ancient gods who had protected the Roman Empire from the time before there was a Catholic church until its enemies succeeded in burning the capital city of Rome in AD 410.

These critics of the Catholic Church were in effect saying that the Roman Empire had prospered under pagan gods from the second century before Christ until the Goths and other enemies succeeded in destroying Rome. Critics of Christianity further alleged that as punishment for this ingratitude, the tried and tested Roman pagan gods turned their backs on Rome; and less than a century after abandoning Rome's pagan gods, disaster had befallen the Roman Empire. When word reached North Africa that critics of the church were saying Rome fell because Roman leaders and people had embraced Christianity, thus turning their backs on the traditional Roman gods, St. Augustine felt a need to answer this historical lie. After reflecting on this matter, and studying available historical evidence for thirteen years, he finally responded to the church's critics by publishing, in serial form, his masterful *City of God. City of God* (St. Augustine)

Augustine said in that great book that there are things temporal and things spiritual. All things on earth are temporal products of history and will eventually be worn down and destroyed by the corrosive forces of history. Things spiritual, on the other hand, are not subject to destruction by the passage of time and the corrosive forces of history. Augustine reminds readers that when God made heaven and earth, He gave man dominion over earth, but not over heaven. Augustine did a search of Holy Scripture to show that God promised from the beginning that the eternal city of heaven will last forever. He relied heavily on the Old Testament to support his conviction that heaven would last forever.

In Augustine's view, the fall of Rome in AD 410 had nothing to do with the fact that its leaders had embraced Christianity a century earlier. Even when Rome remained steadfast in its worship of the ancient

Roman gods, it had suffered many calamities. Augustine provided much detailed information about Rome's triumphs and defeats to support his thesis that the old Roman gods had been powerless to save Rome from defeat. It was clear that the old gods never had the power that defeated Romans were now trying to ascribe to them. Augustine said the eternal city of God exists in heaven and will endure forever. Instead of relying on false gods, Augustine reminds his readers that a much better foundation for one's faith is the truth put forth by the fortieth Psalm: "Blessed is the man whose hope is the Lord God and who respected not vanities and lying follies." In any event, Saint Augustine asked "whether the great extent of the Roman Empire, which was acquired only by wars, is to be reckoned among the good things either of the wise or the happy."

One evening in 1978, when Freddie Mae and I were having dinner at the home of friends from the local *ecole secondaire*, or high school, located in the historic city of Carthage, Tunisia, North Africa, I remarked to dinner guests that Saint Augustine had attended secondary school during the latter part of the fourth century in their fair city of Carthage. The wife and cohost for the dinner, whose beautiful home was located in Carthage, said the school Saint Augustine attended was still located in Carthage in the same old buildings and even had the "same faculty." Did she mean that the teachers lived a very long time? I don't think so. What she probably meant was that the curriculum and buildings had not changed much since Augustine attended secondary school in the ancient and conservative city of Carthage.

From the time I first began to read some of the great books of St. Augustine, I have come to appreciate more and more his grasp of reality. Further, the more I read his writings, the more I was inclined to think that this religious priest, bishop, and man of God of the fourth and fifth centuries AD had much to say that ought to be studied by modern-day men and women.

I traveled where Jesus had walked and lived, and I realized that His followers in what is now known as the Catholic Church had just about as many shortcomings as I had, yet they kept the faith. I was amazed at the grace shown by the nuns who worked in the leprosy colony under deplorable conditions, and I was led to a spiritual awakening by becoming acquainted with the work and writings of the great St. Augustine. With all these personal explorations in Africa and the Middle East, I was bent in the direction of the Catholic Church. Yet there was more examining to be done.

Sixteenth Street Unitarian Church

When I arrived back in the United States from a two-year assignment in Jordan in 1970, I still considered myself a Methodist, and I attended several Methodist churches in an effort to find one where I felt comfortable. I even started visiting churches of other denominations, and that is how I began to attend the Sunday services on a regular basis at the Sixteenth Street Unitarian Church where the well-known Washington minister Rev. David Eaton was senior pastor. After a few weeks, I began to feel quite at home in the Unitarian church.

However, one Sunday morning, Rev. Eaton shocked me and, no doubt, others in the congregation, by announcing that "this is the last Sunday we will use the Lord's Prayer as part of our worship service." Rev. Eaton then repeated the Lord's Prayer phrase by phrase and said,

"We no longer really believe this." For example, he said, "Give us this day, our daily bread. Probably no one in this church believes his daily bread comes from a God who is in heaven. Thy kingdom come, Thy will be done on earth as it is in heaven. Do we really believe God wills all of the evil we see around us in the world today?" Surely we do not was what seemed to be the message he was conveying.

"Forgive us our trespasses as we forgive those who trespass against us," he continued. The eloquent minister spoke of the rising tide of lawsuits we bring against those who commit torts against us or our property. Our actions show that we no longer believe in that part of the Lord's Prayer, he suggested. When Rev. Eaton finished his scrutiny and analysis of the Lord's Prayer, he once again said that this was the last Sunday on which the Lord's Prayer would be used as a part of the worship service. By the time Rev. Eaton completed his message that Sunday morning, I knew that it was time for me to look for another church. I had been taught the Lord's Prayer by my late grandma Mame as soon as I could talk, and I was not prepared to give up what I considered part of the bedrock of my upbringing and faith.

So I arranged a conference with the senior pastor at St. Theresa Catholic Church to see if that church would be running a Roman Catholic Initiation for Adults (RCIA) class anytime soon for candidates who wished to convert to Catholicism. Arrangements were quickly made for me to attend a special class. The senior pastor turned me over to a youthful priest who looked like he had not been out of the seminary very long. I began to go to him once each week for several months for instruction.

Eventually, that priest felt that we had covered the required materials and that I was ready to become a good Catholic. At my request, arrangements were made for me to be baptized into the Catholic Church on my forty-sixth birthday on March 20, 1971. My good friends Mr. and Mrs. Wilbert Smith served as godparents and witnesses. Freddie Mae and I arranged a "birthday and conversion party" to which we invited many of my National War College classmates as well as old friends from undergraduate days at Howard University. Quite a few friends actually expressed surprise that I would convert from Methodism to Catholicism. Contrary to what they may have expected, I have been happily serving God as a Catholic since 1971.

Chapter 17

Closing

I find it remarkable that although I was born into poverty in a small town in North Carolina six months after my father died, I had traveled over much of the world. With the help of a loving grandmother who literally drummed into me, from the age of two years, that if I worked hard, attended church regularly, got all the education possible, I would do well in spite of the legal, social, and economic barriers into which I was born. I believe that Grandma would be proud that I was able to rise to the level of holding prestigious positions throughout the world, ride back and forth to work in chauffeur-driven cars, and dine on fine food in some of the world's finest restaurants. For her sound advice and her spiritual presence within me, I will forever be grateful.

Since I made it out of such a poor and problem-ridden childhood, I fail to be sympathetic when I see youngsters, white, black, or brown, who cannot move from the bottom of the economic and social ladder in America to carve out a slice of the American pie. In my travels around the world, I did not find another country that is as open to improvement for a youngster of poor to moderate means. I find it hard to fathom why so many young people today seem to have wandered off the right path into a life of drugs and incarceration in spite of the magnificent opportunities available to them in education and employment. I believe, as Grandma Mame taught me, that if young men and women prepare themselves to be productive workers, they will find places in society where they can do socially significant work that will be financially rewarding.

In my retirement, I continue to be active in the Catholic Church, particularly Saint Joseph in Holly Springs, Mississippi. Since I became a member of this congregation in 1984, I have served as president of the pastoral council, grand knight of the local chapter of the Knights of Columbus, Eucharistic minister, member of the finance committee, choir member, keeper of the grounds, and all-around volunteer. However, in giving of my time, talents, and treasure to the church, I know that I have received far more than I gave. I intend to keep up my ministry of volunteering for whatever needs to be done by a layman until poor health forces me to cut back my voluntary activities at the church.

I will continue until I receive the command to quit this mortal state. I will await the Second Coming of Christ, secure in the knowledge that at the appointed hour, I will be called forth from bodily corruption to live forever with those who love the Lord and their neighbors as themselves.

References And Notes

Chad. Fort Lamy. *Http://us-africa.tripod.com/chad.html.* January 15, 2005.

CIA. *The World Factbook.* Washington, DC, 2004. *Http://www.cia. gov./cia/publications/factbppl/geos/li.html.*

Cuttington University. Cuttington University, Liberia, West Africa. July 24, 2005. Http://www.cuttington.org/.

Family members. Taped interview. Family members talked without identifying themselves. Occasion was family reunion of Fullington, Hunter, McCoy, Gordon, and Stratmon families. Interview occurred at home of Mrs. Emily Hunter-Fullington. Interview focused on what older family members recalled about Frank C. Gordon and his wife, Nan Gordon, who were great-grandparents of the author and Emily Fullington. New Smyrna Beach, Florida. August 9, 1978.

Gillain, Phillippe. E-mail received on December 13, 2004, from Phillippe Gillain, curator of Museum December '44. Mr. Gillain responded to my e-mail dated 12 December 2004 inquiring about the temporary cemetery the 3128th QM Service Company worked in during 1944-45 where we buried American soldiers felled during the advance of the US Army into Germany in the final rounds of World War II. *Museum@decembre44.com.*

Harper, Jimmie. "Uncle Frank Gordon Taught School for Fifty-Five Years." *State Port Pilot.* Southport, North Carolina. October 30, 1953.

Lee, Eva V. Taped three-hour interview. Atlantic Beach, North Carolina. February 27, 1979.

Matthew 17:14-20. The details of Christ's healing of an epileptic as he and his disciples were coming down from the Mount of Transfiguration.

Prairie View A&M University. *http://www.pvamu.edu/.*

St. Augustine. *The Confessions. The City of God. On Christian Doctrine.* Chicago: William Benton, 1952, 127-618.

Tunis, Tunisia. *www.tunisiaonline.com/government).*

Index

D

Davis, Jack 105
DEAR Realty 159
doctoral dissertation 58
"Doll" 22
Dosher, J. Arthur 26
Douglas, Will 154
DW Estates Subdivision 167

E

Early Church Fathers 180
Eason, John 81
Eaton, David 183
epilepsy 120
Evans, Dollie 31

F

faculty member (Rust College) 55
Fitzhugh, H. Naylor 81
Fort Bragg induction center 52, 69
Fort Lamy. *See* N'Djamena, Chad
Fulbright-Hayes Program 110, 137, 141

G

Ghana 99, 105
Ghana-America Society 107
Gold Coast, West Africa 99, 101, *See
    also* Ghana and Accra, Ghana
  American scholarship 104
  job offer in 96
  leaders of 103, 105
  Gordon

Cenelius 29, 30, 33, 34
Eloise 21, 30
Evelyn 29, 36, 37, 39, 41
Florence 31, 41, 42
Frank 42, 44, 45
Judy 39, 42
Mary Martha McCoy 29, 32, 33, 35
Gray, Albert 164
Griffin, Richard 28
Guerrero
  Jeanne 92
  Lorenzo 92
  Savannah 93

H

Harper, Jimmy 31
Heady, Ferrel 57, 58
Hodges, Courtney 75
Honor Society of Phi Kappa Phi 57
Hotel Bame 28
Howell, Hattie 31
Hunter
  Clyde 23
  Emily 23
  Mabel 22
  Mary Evelyn 23
  William 22

I

induction. *See* Fort Bragg induction
    center
information officer (Kinshasa,
    Congo) 130

Institute of Public Administration
(University of Michigan) 57
Israeli kibbutzim 132

J

Jay Hawk. *See* Henri-Chapelle
American Cemetery
jazz music 107
Jesse H. Jones Rotary House
International 97
John Hay Whitney Foundation, 58
Jordan, Dwan 91

K

kibbutzim. *See* Israeli kibbutzim
King, Martin Luther 102
assasination of 134
Kinshasa, Congo 130, 132

L

Leander, David 21
Lederle, John 57
leprosy colony 178
Lewis, Mark 125
Liberia
brief description of 83
slavery in 84
little white sisters of Africa 178

M

Maronite Catholic community 60
McCoy
Charles Nelson 24, 34, 51
Edward E. \ 32

Joseph 24
Josie Mae 34
Nelson 34
Viola Oly 33
McMillan, W.A. 161
Meisel, James 180
Merriem. *See under* adoptees,
Stratmon, Wassila Merriem
Bourguiba
Mills, Mary Lee 88
Monrovia, Liberia 81
Montgomery, Bernard 75

N

N'Djamena, Chad
arrival in 112
brief description of 112
cultural affairs in 114
cultural attraction in 116
up-country in 118
National Museum of African Art
125, 129
Nkrumah, Kwame 99, 102, 105

P

Parchman Farm 165
Parchman prison. *See* Parchman Farm
Parker, Carl 167
Patton, George 75
pearl of the Middle East. *See* Beirut,
Lebanon
personal assistant (Crown Savings
Bank) 54
poor relief 35